The Blue Sky Bends Over All

A celebration of ten years of the
Immrama Festival of Travel Writing

Lismore, County Waterford

An anthology of essays by participants in the
Immrama Festival during the first decade 2003-2011

Edited by Paul Clements

Published by the
Immrama Travel Writing Festival Committee, 2012

Editorial Selection © Paul Clements and Jan Rotte, 2012
Individual essays © the essayists, 2012
First published 2012

Cover image: artwork used with the permission of Andrea Jameson

The right of Paul Clements to be identified as the editor
of this work has been asserted in accordance with the
Copyright, Designs and Patents Act, 1988.

ISBN 978-0-9572598-0-5

Acknowledgements

The publishers and editor wish to thank the participants who kindly gave of their time to write the essays collected in this book. Special thanks to Andrea Jameson for providing the cover artwork. We are grateful to *The Irish Times* for permission to reproduce the essay by Dervla Murphy, to *The Globe and Mail* for permission to reproduce the essay by Hadani Ditmars and to the editor of the online travel magazine *Perceptive Travel* for permission to reproduce Michael Shapiro's essay.

Printed by Dargan Press, 15 Michelin Road, Mallusk, Newtownabbey BT36 4PT

Contents

Introduction

Dear Friends,

"A very sincere welcome to the Lismore Festival 2003, titled Immrama (an old Irish word for journey), dedicated to the art of travel writing, good music and fine entertainment. The committee, with due regard for the history and heritage of Lismore, has I believe created a festival of outstanding quality and the events listed in this programme will confirm this belief. Over the centuries many people have made journeys to and from Lismore and I hope that you will enjoy your Immram in Lismore. On behalf of the committee and myself, we wish to express our most sincere thanks for the generous support, help and encouragement that we have received from day one in bringing this festival to life. To all those who have come to entertain and be entertained I hope you will have enjoyed your visit to Lismore, and all that this very special place has to offer.

Yours most sincerely on behalf of all at Immrama."

This opening welcome to Immrama in 2003 continues to this day as we bring year ten to life. The first year was a very difficult one for the committee, but a lot was learnt from it, a need to plan better, watch the budget and be focused on what was needed to make following years the success it became. We are committed to presenting a festival of quality dedicated to the art of travel writing and always conscious that it is community based in the heritage town of Lismore where it came to life.

Over the years many great and talented people from the world of travel writing have come to Lismore and have given great pleasure and entertainment to the audiences who come year after year from Ireland, England or further afield such as Canada and Australia. The different theme of each festival attracts a diverse audience. Many of them come for the weekend and contribute much to the business life in both Lismore and West Waterford. The committee is grateful for the financial support that Immrama receives each year, without which the festival could not be possible and for the venues that are made available to the festival.

Over the past nine years the festival and committee have been an "Immrama" of their own. Now they come to year ten and a huge effort has been put into the planning for 2012. It promises to be a year to remember and as always the committee is grateful to all who made each year's Immrama possible. I wish safe travel to all who come to be part of Immrama, especially on this tenth year.

Peter Dowd, President of Immrama

Our journey with Immrama started on a damp autumn evening in 2002 around a table in the Lismore Hotel. A group of us got together to plan a high quality international standard tourism event for Lismore. We got the money together to engage Fidelma Mullane of Galway to draw up a feasibility study for us. Out of that work came the concept of a Travel Writing Festival centred on the fact that Dervla Murphy was born in Cappoquin and lives in Lismore. There was immediate buy-in by the group and we started planning straightaway. We had decided on some musical events to accompany the travel writing component of the festival. We selected a weekend in June and laid plans for the first Immrama.

The content of the first year was excellent and the musical component was very good. However, the box office was disappointing and we lost money. The committee members were quite demoralized by this experience but were determined to keep the momentum of Immrama going. We concentrated on the travel writing events only and at the end of the second year we had made a small surplus. This gave us the template for all future Immrama Festivals.

We established two annual fund-raising events, the table quiz in January and the Devonshire Day in March both of which have become fixtures in the Immrama calendar. In our third year we were able to engage Michael Palin as the main speaker and we have never looked back.

A huge amount of planning goes into each Immrama Festival and the small but hard working committee have never been found wanting. That does not mean that we always agree on everything and never have arguments - we are human too. I have been chairman since 2003 and it is always a pleasure to lead the Immrama Committee from year to year. I get the greatest satisfaction on the closing Sunday evening each year when we congratulate each other on yet another successful Immrama. We enjoy the work immensely. I would like to thank all of the contributors, committee members, sponsors and most importantly the ticket buying audience without whom it would not be possible.

Bernard Leddy, Chairperson of Immrama

Dervla Murphy

I have had an intimate relationship with the Blackwater since my father taught me to swim in 1934 – an important rite of passage, though I can't remember it. Here in West Waterford the river has come a long way from its source near the Cork/Kerry border and is quite close to its Youghal Bay estuary. It flows between steep wooded ridges – sombre in winter, lacy green in spring, heavily green in summer and in autumn a glowing conflagration. To the north, in the near distance, rise the gentle blue curves of the Knockmealdown Mountains.

East and west of Lismore one may walk all day, seeing nobody, through a dog's paradise of woodlands and riverside meadows where the terrain cannot have changed much since the second century. Then, Ptolemy took time off from star-gazing and composed a map of the known world – including the Blackwater, already an important trading route. For lack of Romans, land transport inhibited Irish commerce until comparatively recently.

Gradually, over the decades, nature has wrought numerous changes in this tranquil corner of the Barony of Coshmore and Coshbride. Aged trees have surrendered to gales, or to the slow erosion of their supporting hedgerows, and now lie or lean at odd angles, wearing frills of fungi and housing an abundance of insects. An 18th-century salmon weir has been dismantled by floods. Banks of sand and gravel come and go, creating temporary current-free inlets suitable for teaching small children to swim. Every winter brings certain modifications, usually subtle, but dramatic when great chunks of pastureland are torn away. Other river-bed transformations can seem almost magical, as when a deep, dark, glossy stretch is replaced, within a very few years, by a sparkling amber torrent, shallow enough for its stones to be visible.

In the 1950s and 1960s a dying willow was my diving-board, but it now lies level with the bank, forming a highway for mink – beautiful creatures, though widely and rightly resented. Since their arrival, the swans that habitually nested on the islet near the collapsed weir, just upstream from Lismore castle, have moved house. Responsible swans don't lay eggs within reach of mink. So I can no longer watch the tiny cygnets (little bigger than ducklings) rapidly becoming fawn-grey adolescents. Swan life, being such a joy to watch, encourages anthropomorphism. They seem the ideal family, parents mutually loving and faithful and sharing childcare, adolescents happy to hang out with parents until something hormonal tells them its time to seek a mate.

Otter families are much rarer and even more endearing. In midsummer I like to swim at sunrise, and one year two adults and a juvenile often appeared nearby. If I was already in the water, they ignored me and played: all three having fun, chasing each other, doing gymnastics on a half-submerged fallen branch. Then one would move off to fish for breakfast while the others continued to frolic. It seemed I was no threat while swimming very slowly and quietly. But if they arrived first, and saw me walking towards them, they immediately vanished.

One memorable morning I met an otter on the path, sitting on his haunches, sucking a swan's egg. On an even more memorable morning my dogs interrupted an otter's breakfast by the water's edge – an aberrant otter, no doubt: allegedly, they never catch salmon. That five-pounder became several suppers; I had carried it home furtively, wrapped in colt's-foot leaves, hoping not to be reported to the Duke of Devonshire's bailiff.

Along this valley, on an average day, one sees what I think of as "the quintet": moorhen, duck, cormorant, heron, swan. The cormorants conspicuously colonise a dead elm for several years, then move on, then return. The herons stay put, always building their sprawling, noisome nests in the highest branches of towering sycamores or chestnuts. They are responsible for littering the banks with large horse-mussel shells, once used by the locals as spoon substitutes – a poignant reminder of bygone days when many in this area lived in extreme poverty, while up and down this valley stately homes were being embellished and spacious demesnes expanded.

On lucky days a winged jewel flashes past: kingfishers nest where tangled tree roots protrude from the bank above a semi-stagnant inlet. Occasionally the jewel perches on an alder branch and if I go still, treading water, I may see his lightning dive for something unidentifiable. On other lucky days flocks of wild geese follow the river, their powerful wing music stirring a mysterious emotion, a mix of reverence and diffuse nostalgia. Less common, nowadays, are the iridescent curlew flocks, their plaintive cries not matching their joyous, precisely choreographed swirlings across a wide sky. In recent years a few newcomers have appeared among the cattle: slim, Persil-white egrets, suggesting climate change.

One May afternoon in 1941 I saw something unforgettable. My parents and I were approaching the Blackwater estuary, on our way to Whiting Bay, when suddenly a man waving a red flag leaped out of a ditch. He had probably been dozing; in those days motor traffic merely trickled and our Ford Ten was the only car on the road. Then, before my very eyes, Youghal bridge seemed to disintegrate. Quickly it came apart and a three-mast schooner with an auxiliary engine sailed past us on its way to Cappoquin – or maybe it was going to turn up the Bride with a cargo for Tallow. Twenty years later I was to see from my bicycle saddle one of the last merchant schooners taking advantage of the tide between Camphire and Dromana.

The sight of that splendid vessel sailing upstream, past waving fishermen grouped below Ballintray House, put my father into pedagogic gear. I associated the Blackwater with beauty, silence and solitude, but now I learned about it as a crowded thoroughfare of considerable commercial and military importance. For some 2,000 years, boat and ship-building were a crucial part of riverside life; in the 19th century 50-tonne barges were still being built in such unlikely (to us) places as Ballyduff and Affane. The variety of cargoes carried up and down the Blackwater and Bride indicate how multi-skilled were these communities. Boat-builders, sail-makers, wool-combers and spinners and weavers, stone masons, fishermen, wood-cutters, sand-spreaders, iron smelters, lime burners, leather tanners, basket makers, flour millers, bacon curers, cider brewers, rope makers – each person valued for his or her particular contribution to the local economy. Such people must have enjoyed a high level of self-respect. Now too many of their descendants are reduced to using technologies that minimise physical labour but can't do much for the individual's *amour-propre*.

Seventy years ago children could do their own summertime thing, unconstrained by our era's gruesome alliance between health-and-safety neurotics and compo-culture bandwagoneers. At one stage (aged eight or nine) I developed a craving for rides in carts and sometimes ingratiated myself with the amiable young man who took delivery at the railway station of merchandise for the Wine Vaults, Lismore's main grocery shop. For the many other smaller shops, goods were loaded on handcarts; only the Wine Vaults could afford horse-power. That was an agreeable though too-short ride behind a briskly trotting gelding, a glossy chestnut with a white blaze and an evident sense of his own importance.

More satisfying were the slow four-mile journeys on Patsy Frank's donkey cart, carrying milk to Cappoquin creamery via *Bóthar na Naomh*, said to be Ireland's oldest continually used road. Once upon a time it crossed the Blackwater by the main ford, below the Round Hill. In the 1940s, and long after, it was a pot-holed and deeply rutted boreen, almost overwhelmed in summer by its healthily untamed hedges of ash plants and holly bushes, whitethorn and blackthorn, hazel, elder and crab apple. Through occasional gateways the Blackwater could be glimpsed beyond narrow strips of boggy land, which made Patsy Frank grumpy. Such land could and should be drained, but if the castle wasn't interested no one would bother . . .

"The Castle" was shorthand for the Duke of Devonshire's estate. Infrequently a very old woman (probably much younger than I am now) sought a lift and sat behind the churns wearing a thick black shawl over her head whatever the weather. She must have been among West Waterford's last "shawlies".

Approaching the Blackwater Valley Co-op (opened in 1914), one could smell its milkiness and hear the whirring of separators and the distinctive clatter of churns being scoured before the journey home. Around the creamery it seemed no one ever hurried, and the farmers – wearing cloth caps and calf-length overcoats, their trouser legs bound with twine – held long, animated discussions (sometimes becoming angry arguments) while their animals enjoyed oat nosebags or bundles of hay. What were they discussing? Probably milk prices and politics, themes then closely linked. Nowadays, bureaucrats fix milk prices in distant tower blocks.

On the way home we might pause where *Bóthar na Naomh* is lapped by the Blackwater, and Patsy Frank would light a pipe while gossiping with four nephews who held licences to snap-net salmon just upstream from the Kitchen Hole. Their small, flat-bottomed boats (a model popular over the past 7,000 years) were known as "cots", which for some reason made me giggle – to Patsy Frank's irritation. His father (born in 1852) could remember dozens of cots fishing between old Strancally castle and the Bride Mouth.

Each group of cotmen then had rights to a certain stretch – rights defended, when necessary, with fists. A few famed fishermen were credited with a sixth sense that enabled them to "feel" salmon swimming upstream by night. In 1600, as the New English were tightening their grip, a law banned cots lest insurgents find them useful – this despite so many communities being dependent on fishing. Naturally the cot law was ignored. However, the 1832 cholera epidemic was not ignored; it kept cotmen away from the coast and for months Youghal's merchants had to collect their salmon from Villierstown quay. By then Blackwater salmon – exchanged for silk or wine – had gained renown across Europe.

Traditionally, the men who tended Lismore's salmon hatchery beside the Ownashad (a minor Blackwater tributary) were cot-makers in their spare time. As a 12-year-old I joined the crowd who gathered there one evening to exclaim over a record snap-net catch, a 51-and-a-half pound salmon landed by a four-man cot crew.

That summer I was judged sufficiently mature, mentally and physically, to swim alone in a river I already knew so well. Thereafter my two favourite activities supplemented each other. Cycling allowed me to find various secluded swimming spots between Mocollop, some eight miles west of Lismore, and Villierstown, about the same distance to the east. Downstream from the Kitchen Hole one had to beware of the tide; elsewhere, one had to check for dense underwater weeds.

As a teenager I once swam in the Bride, the Blackwater's main tributary, without first studying its tidal whims. I forget what prompted that lapse into mental immaturity. But I shall never forget my fear when I realised that I could neither swim back to my starting point nor reach the bank. Along that stretch there was no visible bank, only treacherous, muddy reed-beds.

Not until the tide had carried me down to Camphire bridge was I able to scramble ashore, very cold and very shaken. Luckily, haymakers had been near my starting point; otherwise I would have been naked. I set out to hitch-hike back to my belongings and soon a bemused elderly farmer, driving a cart-load of spires to Sapperton, bravely picked me up and hastily wrapped me in sacking. I wasn't the first reckless swimmer to have come ashore at Camphire bridge. The Bride was famous for its reed-beds; to this day one sees a few spires stacked near the bridge. Sadly, people say they have been much weakened by agri-pollution, and for major jobs thatchers must now import from Hungary or Turkey.

Towards the end of the 1950s motor traffic began to replace draft animals, to my great distress. Cyclists dislike sharing roads with other machines. Rapidly the pace of life changed, as did attitudes to farming, which around then became the "agricultural industry" – an ominous semantic shift. (Similarly, publishing became the "book industry", to the great detriment of non-bestselling authors.) By 1965 very few milk suppliers were driving carts to the creamery.

West Waterford disappoints some of my foreign guests. They protest, 'It's too like Sussex or Dorset, too unlike Kerry or Donegal'. I see their point, yet to me West Waterford, south Tipperary and east Cork are incomparably satisfying. Everything is congenial: every curve of the hills and valleys, every bend of the rivers and streams, every distinctive seasonal scent of fields and woods. This territory is my natural habitat, where I'm at ease in all weathers. It doesn't do to forget that we too are animals, albeit with certain unique capabilities increasingly lethal to our fellow animals.

As for the natural beauties of Lismore, they are scarcely to be surpassed. The Blackwater, both above and below the bridge which leads into the town, flows through one of the most verdant of valleys, just wide enough to shew its greenness and fertility; and diversified by noble single trees, and fine groups...Nothing I say, can surpass, in richness and beauty, the view from the bridge, when at evening, the deep woods, and the grey castle, and the still river, are left in shade; while the sun, streaming up the valley, gilds all the softer slopes and swells that lie opposite. To say that there are no unemployed poor, and no beggars, or paupers in Lismore, would be, to assert an untruth; but I feel myself bound to say, that of the former, class there are comparatively few; and that a large proportion of the pauperism of Lismore, does not naturally belong to it; but has resulted from the *clearances* of some neighbouring, and less considerate landlords.

Henry D. Inglis, *Ireland in 1834*

Tim Butcher

Graham Greene, the English author whose best work was born of travel, got his timing wrong for his first visit to Waterford. He was just 18 and on the 'long vac' from Oxford (Being from a family of privilege he can be forgiven for using that sort of language) when he hiked from Dublin to Waterford in the summer of 1923. He might have been young but he did not suffer from lack of confidence, soon after placing an article in the weekly *Westminster Gazette* giving his impressions on newly independent Ireland. The writer who would make a name as the diviner of all things seedy dwelled, needless to say, on the negative: "beggars on Grafton Street, an air of apathetic expectation and unspeakable liver and bacon served in a backstreet restaurant". If only he had waited 90 years or so, then he would have had a dramatically different experience at the Immrama travel writing festival.

My memory of arriving in Lismore is one of green. It was 2008 and I was then living in the Middle East on top of the Mount of Olives overlooking that most ancient and disputed of cities, Jerusalem. It was scorching high summer in the Judean desert so I had seen scarcely a green frond in months. To approach up and through the Vee and look down into Lismore was giddy-making. How many richer hues of green can there be? You have to know that I was brought up a keen fly fisherman so to walk over the bridge and find an angler casting into the clear, brown current of the river below the battlements of the castle was, once more, enough to make me stop in awe. Can there be a more perfect setting for fly-fishing?

The weekend was a blur of well-organised, book-focused indulgence with a rolling programme of great events punctuated by warm hospitality. The last time I had seen my journalist colleague Christina Lamb was in the Baluchi tribal buffer zone between

Pakistan and Afghanistan but there she now was on Main Street, Lismore. Oddly for a woman who has worked in war zones she looked more nervous than ever as she entered the Courthouse Theatre for one of her events.

The following morning and a radio DJ was in town, or to be more precise a caravan carrying a mobile radio studio parked on Main Street. All us 'artists' had a slot of airtime in my case squeezed between the travel and a track by the Cure. It's a pretty rich radio audience that can cope in the same stanza with roadworks on the N72 and a self-publicist banging on and on about the Congo. My ego was brought down to earth a little later after a run over to Dungarvan where the hugely enthusiastic owner of the local branch of the Eason bookshop chain had me sitting outside his shop at a table weighed down with my books. You don't know loneliness like the loneliness of an author being ignored in a shopping centre. It's just you and the tumbleweed. Bless the teenage girl who put me out of my misery. "It's Father's Day soon so I will have one for my Dad," she said, offering me a copy to sign.

The shopowner's enthusiasm was undiminished and he was proved right later that day when I spoke in the Courthouse. An audience who clearly loved both books and travel filled the place and business was brisk when it came to signing. For me the best book events are the ones where one learns something. The subject of my 2008 book was a journey I did in the Congo, one that made me fairly knowledgeable on matters Congo, not least the troubled deployment of Irish soldiers there as United Nations peacekeepers in the early 1960s. It was a subject I had read much about but the thrill of Immrama was to meet two local men who had actually been on that mission. That was the moment to turn one's internal radio from broadcast to receive so I could thrill in their recollections and anecdotes.

Graham Greene would not have recognized the food. The only argument Jane and I had all weekend was over our choice of eatery. And when we eventually left Lismore our toughest challenge was working out how to smuggle black pudding from the High Street butcher past the sniffer dogs at Ben Gurion airport (hide them in a man's three-day-worn socks is the answer, if you are interested).

The festival was big enough to have a critical mass of great audiences and engaging events (Redmond O'Hanlon's fertility symbols made for a Ballyrafter breakfast of particular engagement) without being too cumbersome or self-important. It struck the perfect balance.

My self-importance was brought nicely back to earth during my event at the Courthouse. It fell to Edward, the town vet, to both introduce me and to give the vote of thanks at the end. During my talk I noticed out of the corner of my eye a bit of a fuss as Edward slipped out and back. "What happened there?" I asked after the event. "I had a text message from a client with a cow that had developed problems. Your talk was important but I had to do something, so I had him bring the cow in a trailer and I treated outside. I was back in time for the vote of thanks – nobody's the wiser."

The approach to Lismore is picturesque and beautiful. The river ceases to be navigable at a short distance from Cappoquinn…The canal runs for some miles through a finely planted pleasure ground and the castle, high above the level of the water, is kept in view nearly all the way, and crowns a landscape that is at once magnificent and graceful. The castle is situated on a steep rock which rises perpendicularly from the river. To look down from one of its chamber windows would make the clearest head dizzy, and there is a tradition that James II darted back in terror when he was conducted to a lattice to take a view of the surrounding scene. There are no fewer than forty-two salmon weirs on the Blackwater between Youghal and Lismore; the one immediately under the castle is the last and most productive, where it is by no means rare to take 600 fish at a first haul. The fishery is rented from the Duke by Mr Foley at a rental, we are informed, of £700 per annum…Lismore is but a few hours from Waterford, and Waterford is but twenty hours' sail from Bristol…though of late years it has dwindled to a rank scarcely above that of a village, time was when it could vie in importance with the most flourishing city in Ireland, having once been a university and a bishop's see.

Hall's Ireland, Mr & Mrs Hall's Tour of 1840

Nuala Hayes

I didn't think twice when the invitation came. Would I come to Lismore and tell stories? Does a bird fly? My heart lifts. I love the word Immrama. It's a perfect name for a festival of travel writing. *Iomradh*, in old Irish: a journey, a voyage of the imagination, a trip away from everyday reality.

The monastic scribes who penned *Iomrama*, those poetic stories of voyages across the sea, to islands both real and imagined, could have been the first travel writers. The first story I learnt to tell was *Iomradh Bhran*, the Voyage of Bran MacFeabhal, to *Imchúin*, the Land of Women. It is one of the most ancient of Irish Tales, a 'perfect pagan' story, according to Douglas Hyde. Maybe that might be a story too for Lismore in June during the celebration of travel and writing.

How to get there from Dublin? The directions were clear. Take the road to Cork and turn left after Cashel and follow the road through the Vee. If you are to traverse the Vee for the first time, June is the perfect month. The rhododendrons are in full bloom and every twist and turn through the mountain gap reveals a sight that is so glorious you want to stop and stay forever. It flashes past and the next turn reveals another, even better view. You drive past the rag-bedecked sacred bush and you wonder, what's the story there?

Then way down in the valley you see a lake and you have to stop. It's dark and deep and ominous. There's a track leading to it and a statue…so there must be another story. There is indeed. I've passed Baylough, the lake associated with Petticoat Loose – I'd heard about her and her wild ways. An independent woman. The early Church, as we know, had no time for such trollops. An archbishop confronted her once and asked what was in her basket? Pups, she answered brazenly. Open the basket, the holy man demanded. She did, and inside were no puppies, but babies, seven of them! All boys, all alive! Give me the babies he said, and I'll bring them up to be holy men.

The Blue Sky Bends Over All

He banished her to Baylough, by the old road across the Knockmealdown Mountains. She used to travel the road hitching lifts and it was said, although she was thin as a rake, if you took her in your cart, the weight of her sins would put the horses in a lather of sweat. Petticoat Loose met her end in a watery grave in that dark lake. Sometimes at night, they say, a green beam shoots out from the lake and you can see her hand with a thimble on her index finger. Folklore embellishes and leaves the facts to the imagination.

The sun was setting as I reached the comfort of Ballyrafter House and my room for the night. The welcome was warm and the view across the Blackwater River to the castle was spectacular. There was excitement in the air. Participants were gathering; exotic and experienced travellers and journalists, with photographs and books to prove it. I feel a bit empty-handed, but the stories are in my head and I love to listen to other people's adventures from the comfort of a seat by the fire.

Next day, I walked into town, over the bridge and the river, and if I were an auctioneer, I'd say: location, location, location. They knew what they were doing, these people of olden times who chose this spot for the *Lios*, the ancient fort that gives Lismore its name; as did the monks, the builders of monasteries and the scribes of the Annals.

Planters and colonists always chose a place from where they could defend themselves and the castle to this day has a sense of the impenetrable about it. It seems to be from another world, another time for another people. The footprints of history are everywhere in Lismore and that's what makes it so fascinating. As does the palpable pride of the residents who love to share its story with visitors.

I found the library, with Dervla Murphy's famed bicycle mounted on the wall. We told stories outside, sitting under a tree on Saturday morning and imagined the branches above us were full of monkeys. I did eventually release my story of the Voyage of Bran, but maybe not in a context the eighth century scribe who wrote it down could ever imagine. This was 2003, and the building boom in Ireland was in full swing. Our venue was a popular pub in the town. The bar was packed with Russian and Polish construction workers on their night off from building houses in the new estates on the outskirts. They are in lively form and they do their best to show interest when Louis de Paor recites his poetry *as Gaeilge*. But when I begin my saga of the hero, Bran Mac Feabhail, who is beguiled by a woman from the otherworld to take to his currachs with his band of men and search the seas for her, the Russians and Poles just don't get it…at first.

Then Hadani Ditmars the Canadian journalist and writer, saves the night. She is possessed, not alone of great beauty, but of a mixture of genes which gives her Lebanese, French, Russian, and I'm sure Polish ancestry too. She can sing in all these languages, play the guitar and dance at the same time. The pub falls silent, then cheers erupt and the visiting workers from Russia and Poland now understand at last what the Voyage of Bran is all about.

The beautiful Blackwater river suddenly opened before us, and driving along it for three miles through some of the most beautiful, rich country ever seen, we came to Lismore. Nothing can be certainly more magnificent than this drive. Parks and rocks covered with the grandest foliage; rich, handsome seats of gentlemen in the midst of fair lawns, and beautiful bright plantations and shrubberies; and at the end, the graceful spire of Lismore church, the prettiest I have seen in, or, I think, out of Ireland. Nor in any country that I have visited have I seen a view more noble – it is too rich and peaceful to be what is called romantic, but lofty, large, and *generous*, if the term may be used; the river and banks as fine as the Rhine.

William Makepeace Thackeray, *Irish Sketch Book*, 1842

Donald Brady

My first visit to Waterford was as a delegate to an assistant librarians conference held at the Ardree Hotel in the city. My recollections of that visit are centred on a wonderful night in Katie Reilly's Kitchen and a subsequent chance meeting with Val Doonican who was staying at the Ardree. However, it was Dervla Murphy who provided my first impressions of this wonderful county and particularly the area of West Waterford and its historic capital Lismore.

I had applied for the post of County Librarian and a colleague strongly advised me to peruse *Wheels within Wheels*. Not only did this book create an immediate interest and enthusiasm for the area but in its descriptions of the creation of the county library service and its first librarian, Dervla's father Fergus, I was introduced to one of the most inspirational and influential figures that the public library service has ever seen. In his background, as a participant in the 1916 Rebellion and in the subsequent fight for Irish Freedom, Fergus displayed deep-seated altruism, self-sacrifice and a commitment to the common good, characteristics which later generated one of the finest services in the country.

Following my appointment, I had to wait for almost six months before I had a chance encounter with Dervla one early afternoon in Lismore as, in the company of her dogs, she returned home. An immediate invitation was issued to her house and several hours later after a discussion, lubricated by several beers, which incorporated impressions of both our travels, the library service and of course Waterford, I left in rather good form and delighted with a new and as it happened long-standing friendship.

The Immrama Festival provided me with a tremendous opportunity to research, and a unique forum to present, findings on subjects which I felt were of major local interest.

My first presentation was on Henry Grattan Flood, a native of Lismore and a man whose work on the history of Waterford, his major contribution to national musicology and his musical compositions, have earned him a singularly appropriate memorial in his adopted town of Enniscorthy, but unfortunately little recognition at home. My later contributions on the Boyle family and the unique Lismore Papers reflect a personal fascination as do presentations made on film and film-making and film director William Desmond Taylor. However, my presentation on *The Book of Lismore* was entirely due to the suggestion of the festival committee and specifically the driving vision of Mary Houlihan.

Exploration of this work opened my eyes to an extraordinary anthology of Celtic medieval scholarship and the evolution of this paper into a book has, I hope, provided a lasting legacy to one initiative of the festival organisers. A hurriedly produced and incomplete listing of the authors of the county, launched as part of the Festival, with the title *The Writers of County Waterford* provided some satisfaction and recognition of my role as a bibliophile. But it was the most eloquent introduction and launch of the book by local poet Thomas McCarthy, in the appropriate setting of the recently completed library headquarters which gave me the deepest satisfaction.

During the early years of the festival I was privileged to host several of the speakers on behalf of the committee. With Brid Rodgers, deputy leader of the SDLP (Social Democratic and Labour Party) I had an immediate rapport. Not only were we fellow Northerners but we shared a passion for the Donegal Gaeltacht, birthplace of Brid and more critically a life-long interest in Civil Rights. We shared recollection of the march held in Newry on 6 February 1972. This took place "exactly a week after Derry's Bloody Sunday." Because of the events the previous week it became the "biggest ever Civil Rights march." Over 80,000 attended and saw the day as "a vindication of their stand against the slaughter of the pervious Sunday." I was one of the few from the South to attend that march. I brought Brid on a short tour of Lismore which concluded with a visit to the recently completed new library headquarters and its highlight, the beautifully restored oratory of the Brothers which now serves as the office of the County Librarian.

I shared significant memories with Jon Halliday, husband of Jung Chang. His father in 1928 purchased the "defunct Celt Boot Company in Quay Street Dundalk..." and established the shoe firm of Halliday & Son which, at its zenith, employed 1,250 people. Jon and his brothers were partly educated in the local Marist College attended by my father. The contribution of Jon's late brother Fred to the local cultural environment is well known as illustrated by a report in the local newspaper *The Argus* on 15 April 2005:

Orange met green in the unique setting of Louth County Museum
on Friday evening last at the opening of an exhibition on the
Orange Order by the British Ambassador Stewart Eldon.
Also present was Robert Saulters Grand Master of the
Orange Order…

The paper also related that a seminar, "Cultural Identity – Changing Perceptions" held at Dundalk Institute to coincide, had a keynote address given by Fred Halliday.

I have had for years a huge interest in Russian literature and society. Its literature displays a movement from rural and ascendancy based culture as exemplified by the work of authors such as Tolstoy and Chekhov through to a revolutionary, urban and largely industrial based literary landscape as depicted by Dostoevsky, Gogol and Gorky. These movements are singularly paralleled in the development of Irish literature and I was delighted to have the opportunity to meet and discuss my impressions with Alexandra Tolstoy distant cousin of the author of *War and Peace*.

Michael Palin, in the delightful surroundings of the Ballyrafter Hotel, proved the most amiable of companions. On a most sociable evening in Madden's pub, I discovered that Charlie Bird had begun his career under the tutelage of Pat O'Connor as part of the *Seven Days* team. Brian Keenan and Hadani Ditmars were likewise extraordinarily stimulating company and I will always treasure the inscription by Fergal Keane on my copy of his book, *All of These People*. ("To Donald: A man with a sacred job – I admire librarians – they are part of what keeps us civilized."). The Molly Keane Awards, instituted by Arts Officer Margaret Organ, have provided a highlight in Lismore library each year.

But despite all these memories, perhaps my most enduring and indelible recollection concerns the committee chairman Bernard Leddy and his annual Trojan efforts to ensure that his programme is signed by all of the contributors. With his enthusiasm and that of all the committee, I have little doubt that Immrama will continue to be an essential event for all those interested in travel writing and literature in general.

When my guide had conducted me to Lismore, and showed me into the celebrated church, which in the days of the never-forgotten Cromwell was defaced, and taken possession of by the Protestants, he abruptly took leave, saying, "I have showed ye all I can." I stood alone in the midst of that venerable pile, looking at its pictures and stained glass windows, through which the setting sun shed a mellow light, throwing upon its walls a softened sadness, which, as the flickering rays died away, seemed to say, "The glory of Erin is departed." The town was in high glee, for O'Connell was liberated. One of the newspaper editors who had been imprisoned with him was there, and bonfires blazed in various places, their smoke giving to the tasteful little town the appearance of a reeking furnace.

Asenath Nicholson,
Ireland's Welcome to the Stranger: or Excursions through Ireland in 1844 & 1845, 1847

Áine Uí Fhoghlú

The first year I was invited to participate in the Immrama Festival coincided with the first summer after a lapse of many years that I decided to accommodate students who come to the Gaeltacht every year to learn or improve their Irish. Many finishing touches had to be added to our newly-built house and an earnest *cigire* (inspector) paid numerous visits in the run-up to ensure that our standards were adequate.

After frantic final preparations, and then the 14 arrivals, numerous cups of steaming tea and home made brown scones were served to parents anxious to establish that their offspring would be well looked after during the coming three weeks. Leaving others to entertain for a while I slipped upstairs to finalise my notes and photocopies for the following morning's poetry workshop in Lismore library.

The first Friday morning in June and the teenage students got their initial view of a honeyed sun emerging from the sea off Helvic just east of their bedroom windows. It would be a fine day. Breakfast dishes cleared away, my daughter took over and I set off for Lismore to begin my first of three workshops with local primary schoolchildren.

Notes: check; photocopies: check; CDs: check; CD player: check; pages torn from *National Geographic*: check. My kit complete I laid it on the front passenger seat and left my mobile phone on top of it. The sun was at my back as I made my way north-west along by the wide stretch of the River Blackwater after Cappoquin. The morning was calm, the river seemed still and the lush growth and cloudless sky were mirrored in the waterway named after the fertility goddess. Its official name: *An Abha Mhór* (the big river) but according to the great old Munster song *Abha Móire*, the river of *Mór*, the Celtic goddess. Along with thoughts of ancient travellers using this waterway, came flooding into my mind the story of the seventh century saint Mochuda or Cárthach who with his band of followers made their way from Rathan in Co. Offaly to the banks of this great river and established their monastery on the hill where now stands the Norman castle.

Immrama was a travel-writing festival. It occurred to me that the journey from the borders of ancient Meath to Lismore in 635 AD must have been at least as arduous and formidable as Dervla Murphy's travels in the Andes but without the benefits of modern research and route-planning gadgetry. I imagined the monks in their beetle-shell coracles navigating parallel to where I was now driving and remembered what I had learned in school about the monastery that had made Lismore one of the most important seats of learning in Ireland for a period of four centuries.

Looking up to my right as I approached the town I imagined the monastic settlement. Its many huts and structures were said to have stretched for nine miles along the river bank. It is recorded as a city of learning, akin to a modern university city with a booming economy. My mind recreated scribes in the scriptorium stooped over their vellum pages as they copied the scriptures, recorded history, wrote down sagas, poems, martyrologies and secular laws in their most exquisite handwriting. I conjured up images of the attendants whose job it was to grind the roots and semi-precious stones and mix the powders from which to make the pigments for the coloured inks. I imagined abbots and bishops, students and scholars, prayers and pilgrims, cattle and cultivation, the carving of antler into needle and comb, the goldsmith, the silversmith and the bronze worker, the drying and grinding of corn and the mill which must have existed given the mighty force at hand to power it. I thought of the fullers, the spinners, the weavers and the dye-makers. I was approaching the town which once was as powerful as the lost city of the Andes.

I saw the ducks before I saw the sign. Not wishing to abruptly end the lives of the three dreamy waddlers who had sneaked out of the canal unnoticed, I braked hard. My ABS kicked in and my notes, CDs, photocopies, *National Geographic* pictures and phone jerked forward and scattered all over the floor. By perfect mischance at that moment the phone rang – a quick glimpse in the rearview mirror and relief that there was no one behind. Hazard lights on, handbrake pulled, I reached down and found it. The call was from home. "Just a minute," I drove on and pulled in. The *cigire* whose final visit was not expected for another day was in the area so had decided to call on us a day early. It is protocol for the *bean an tí* (woman of the house or person responsible for the care of the students), in this case me, to be there to meet him. Promptly behind him arrived into the yard a minibus full of local schoolchildren and their teacher who were coming to learn about beekeeping, to view an observation hive of honeybees and taste some homemade honey and nut biscuits. "Show the *cigire* the bees," was all I could think of "and give him tea and biscuits."

I was already late. The eager young faces were waiting anxiously to quiz me. They arranged themselves in a semicircle around me on the floor and I began. Pádraig de Brún's 'Valparaiso' was a poem I had loved since my own primary school days. It describes the arrival of a ship from the South American port and the decision by the poet not to accept the invitation to go aboard and sail on an adventure journey to magical places, lands of sunshine and wondrous shores. It is a poem about lost youth and lost opportunities.

A hand shot up: "Why didn't he go to Valparaiso? God! I would if a ship pulled up and invited me." Looking around for approval, my reply was to repeat the question back to the group and a mini-philosophical discussion ensued. It came to their turn to start writing and some promising first-attempts were produced. As I went around the circle helping and encouraging one shy little girl whispered to me: "Where do you get your ideas for your writing?" I crouched down beside her and said that unexpected or unusual experiences were always an inspiration. "Like if a dog ran out in front of a car and you saw it and you were afraid it would be knocked down?" "Yes," I replied. "Or maybe ducks."

I dismissed my car at the "Devonshire Arms," an admirable little hotel near the river, and having ordered my dinner there, walked down to the castle, almost within the grounds of which the hotel stands. The views up and down the Blackwater from the drawing-room windows are simply the perfection of river landscape…The hostess of the "Devonshire Arms" gave me some excellent salmon, fresh from the river, and a very good dinner. She bewailed the evil days on which she has fallen, and the loss to Lismore of all that the Castle used to mean to the people. Lady Edward Cavendish had spent a short time here some little time ago, she said, and the people were delighted to have her come there. "It would be a great thing for the country if all the uproar and quarrelling could be put to an end too. It did nobody any good, least of all the poor people."

William Henry Hurlbert, *Ireland under coercion: the diary of an American*, 1888

Pico Iyer

I'd never been to Ireland until I was invited to the Immrama Festival, and now it seems
as if my wife and I have never left it. In 53 years on the planet, despite having been
born and spent my first 21 years in England, despite having travelled from North Korea
to Easter Island to Ethiopia to Yemen, despite having steeped myself for decades in Van
Morrison and Yeats and U2 and Wilde, I'd never set foot on what I'd long heard to be one
of the most magical islands on earth until I received an invitation to come to Lismore in
2010. Ireland had always been a present I could hold on to for myself, a place to look
forward to.

Yet within a few hours of flying into Cork (from California) and arriving in the
enchantment that is Lismore, Hiroko and I were transported. The light seemed to go on and
on deep into the evening. The roads were as quiet – as well as picturesque – as any I'd seen
in a lifetime of travelling. Lismore Castle sat above us every time we walked into town, and
we were treated to four-course dinners every night in a country-house hotel that contrived
to seem, thanks to Joe and Noreen, at once like home and warm-hearted luxury.

My first evening in Ireland, I was getting to see the legendary Dervla Murphy – usually
to be found only in Ethiopia or Cuba or Tibet – waving a farewell as she fastened the gates
to her sanctuary (to let out what turned out to be, as in a fairy-tale again, two friends of
ours from California who had flown across the world for the festival). My first full day in
town, again as if by magic, I was meeting an old friend who had lived in the same house as
I at school, but whom I hadn't seen in 35 years. He invited us to the other worldly castle
where he was staying, all winding, narrow staircases and little alcoves and mysterious
mementoes, where a smiling, indomitable woman of about our age served us tea (she
turned out to be 87).

The Blue Sky Bends Over All

My wife, more sensible than I am, quickly began to feel that we'd stepped out of real life altogether and into some mystical realm that observed a different kind of logic; without ever knowing of Celtic mists or myths, she remains convinced that she dreamed the whole stay and if we were to go back to the place of tolling bells and riverside walks, we'd never be able to find Castle Dodard again. Our second day in Lismore, two sisters were treating us to a sumptuous lunch and then we were travelling by boat along the river, past beautiful houses sleeping by the water; soon thereafter, we were hearing harrowing stories of Arctic exploration and suffering from the deadpan Ranulph Fiennes, and meeting Elizabeth Morris, the wonderful wife of my prose hero since boyhood, Jan.

And the people of Lismore! The local publican and the local vet and kind Ann who drove us all over the rich green landscape (even greener and more full of spirits than legend had moved us to expect) and then took us to a haunting service at a convent (where we met, as if stepping out of a storybook, a lovely nun from Japan). Mary, who ferried us everywhere for day after day, and the two brothers who drove us off to see the ocean and then back to Cork. Everyone at Fort William, which remains the most extraordinary house I've seen, and where we watched horses gallop through golden light above the river and then sat in a tent and listened to Jan Morris as storms shook the world outside.

We bought CDs to try to import something of Ireland into our little two-room flat in rural Japan; we took photographs and notes as a way to make that transfixingly silent and stainless landscape live in the midst of our Buddhist temples and shrines (and almost seem real). I just gave Hiroko an Ireland calendar so that we'll be surrounded by those narrow paths and unspoilt hills through every day of the year to come.

But it's hopeless. None of it can quite capture the hospitality and quiet and genuine friendliness we met every day we were in Lismore's company. Ten years old this year? More like ten thousand. My wife will not be happy until we come back, she hopes for life.

Having passed the twelfth milestone and come in sight of Tallow, the general appearance of the scene became greatly improved; and when, at length, we reached Joyce's well-known establishment our appetites for breakfast would not have helped to make the fortune of any hotel proprietor...Strolling quietly along by the old road, we soon crossed the intervening hills, and reaching Lismore before three o'clock...It was with rebellious spirits, but well loaded pockets, that we cross the Blackwater at the hour named. Anyone who cares for sylvan scenery and who has not as yet visited Lismore, ought to take the first opportunity of doing so. I know of nothing more gently beautiful than the surroundings of this ancient seat of learning; more especially along by the glen, which we were now traversing.

John Herman Rice, *Moonbeams, ca.*,1913

Thomas McCarthy

History has blessed Lismore. Though I am proud to be from 'Cappoquin of the Poets' – that town of the Old Dark Blue rowing eights of my childhood in Twig Bog Lane – I am conscious of the historic centrality of Lismore and its great good ecclesiastical and civil fortune. My Cappoquin has neither a Castle nor an Urban District Council. Lismore has both; and it was the centre of a Poor Law Union in the olden days; so much so that in my childhood 'to be destined for the poorhouse' meant to be Lismore-bound.

But here, also, is the seat of a Bishop: its historic importance is faithfully preserved in the name of our diocese, Waterford AND Lismore. So it demands our respect. In this hallowed place St Carthage, Mochuda, made his peace with the powers of Church and Kings, here the ancient MacCarthys came to pray, to raid or to retire. The Book of Lismore itself, a Book of McCarthy Riabhach, was semi-attached to Lismore, coming and going in raids until it finally found refuge inside the very walls of the town. That this illuminated book, this wedding compilation from ancient times, contains a version of Marco Polo's travels only serves to deliver us into a kind of Lismore prophecy: Lismore has always been a centre-point of Immrama; of voyages outward and emotional returns.

For me, Lismore has always meant Mochuda and Dervla. Dervla, the less historical personage, a voyager and chronicler like the famous Venetian. In many ways she has travelled farther than Marco Polo and with a much smaller retinue of bicycle, donkey and daughter. She has endured landslides, floods, torrents, chasms, storms, spiders and bandits, trekking and cycling from the Andes to the Urals, from sun-baked Coorg to snow-covered Russia. Daughter of Waterford's County Librarian, she fled into an abyss of liberating discomfort:

The river then played a nasty trick by swinging in to the foot of a
sheer mountain, forcing us to ford it again. Beyond another long
stretch of shifting, tiring sand we passed the remains of two ancient
bridges, both of which had crossed the now-dry tributaries just above
their confluence with the Rio Negra. We were still on the wrong side
of the river, which here was deeper and faster…

There she was, in *Eight Feet in the Andes*, far from Lismore, searching for the elusive
Camino Real. She has always meant Lismore to me: through her Lismore extends itself.
Writers can stretch a place, that's part of their function; an unconscious part, yet very real.
Through Dervla Murphy, Lismore extends itself into the imaginations of many thousand
readers. Through such writing Lismore blossoms and becomes re-imagined; as it does with
George O'Brien, another chronicler, a scholar and exile. From his perch at Georgetown
University in Washington DC he has delivered an exquisite trilogy of longing; a veritable
archaeology of Waterford childhood. In *The Village of Longing* Ireland stands still: or time
stands still and allows all our childhoods to rush backward into a vortex of longing.
So, if it isn't Marco Polo, honorary Lismore-man, it is Dervla and Seoirse – or another
Lismore name, a name that conjures an earlier era of great gardeners and Curraghmore
connections: Lady Anson. In *Another Book*, published in 1937, Lady Anson wrote:

Our old herd, Murphy, at Ballysaggart, always got drunk when
he drove cattle or sheep to the fair. One evening when he was
coming home in his donkey cart he was hailed by a tipsy friend
on the road. He pulled at the rope reins, but of course no donkey
will stop when you pull at it, so Murphy made a huge effort. One
of the reins broke, and he fell into the road, the wheel of his own
cart passing over him, breaking most of his bones. I went to see
him and found him sitting uncomfortably on a wooden packing-case
in his cottage all tied up in bandages and splints. He had £800 in the
bank, but it never occurred to him to buy an easy chair or any
necessary furniture; he was keeping the money as a dowry for his
daughter as he wanted her to marry a farmer, he being of farmer class
himself, and in Ireland you cannot marry into a farm without a dowry
so as to pay off the mother-in-law and the sisters-in-law, the latter's
share being used as their dowry, and so on, nobody getting any good
out of the money except the bank…

Mr. Murphy was hardly grateful to the author when her book was published, but you can see that the tradition of memoir and women speaking bluntly is a fine Lismore tradition. That creativity is in Lismore still. Ten years ago when I edited *The Turning Tide*, an anthology of new writing, for Waterford County Council, Lismore was well represented. James Ballantyne, poet of *The Dracula Set* (1993), was present, as was Monica Corfield-Ottman with her very moving Anglo-Indian war story 'Missing in Action...Feared Dead.' Playwright Sylvia Cullen, author of *Chrysalis* and *The Thaw*, was there, as was Íde O Carroll with her haunting 'Georgia O'Keeffe' – *Tháinig mé go hAbiquiu / duitse, Georgia, / le breathnú ar an talamh / tirim seo, / a mheall thú siar / ó Nua-Eabhrac go Nua-Mheicsiceo / ar thóir do chroí is t'anama / 'sna conic seo atá fíor.*

So the creative spirit of a place endures, both in Irish and English. Fiction and poetry seem to rise from the stones, the walls, the flower-beds and bars. The chemistry of Boyle, the schools and almshouse of Sir Walter Raleigh, the cathedral choirs, the dancing of Adele and Fred Astaire, the love-pangs of Sir John Betjeman (who in West Waterford now owns a copy of that love-poem printed for Betjeman by Hogans of Lismore?), all pirouette and cohere around the Castle grounds; all come to rest in a County Library's local studies room. Even imaginatively, *especially* imaginatively, Lismore lives within me: when I published *The Last Geraldine Officer*, very much a Cappoquin book, there were fragments of Lismore everywhere. In a poem 'An Anglo-Irish Luncheon' I imagined being with my father, or father-figure, canvassing for a general election, on Lismore Bridge while the ghosts of this place passed by:

> I was with my father chasing the last seven votes,
> Like a young curate of the old school delivering Repeal Cards,
> When this party of the Belle Assemblée
> Passed us by near Lismore Bridge. It was
> A procession like no other, it was
>
> Fine women carrying the torch of life

Though it is a book of poetry, it does contain four recipes, one of them 'Lismore Castle Cumberland Sauce.' There is also a poem in my book – because the officer is imagined as an Irish language poet – about Micheál Mac Líammóir at Lismore Castle. I must have embellished this from a Mac Líammóir memoir of the period, 1948: '*Bhí leathanta ann agus bhí Lios Mór dathúil-- / Olltoghchán thart, an lucht nua sa Dáil. / Bhuaileas le Micheál i gcomhluadar Clodagh Anson...*'

The poem was an attempt by me to say something about the duality of Lismore, its Gaelic heritage as well as its social modernity in the characters of Adele Astaire or Clodagh Anson. The poet of the Gael, Micheál, was perfectly at home in Lismore Castle, to the manor born in the manner of every poet I know. So it is with Lismore. Through its writers it has extended its reach and influence across the world of serious readers, and through writing the world has flooded in to Lismore like an ancient parchment. Is this not the purpose of journeys; is that not the destiny of all Immrama? Lismore endures in our time as both a place and a place of conversation between happy strangers.

The road that runs due south from Cashel, through Cahir and Clogheen over the mountains to Lismore is one of the most beautiful I have ever travelled. This is one of the grandest views in the British Isles…It is difficult to tear yourself away from such a sight. But the road goes on and up into mountains, bare and barren and brown; then it falls to one of the sweetest glens in the world where a laughing stream runs beside you all the way to Lismore, a delightful, clean, reserved and dignified country town. I was pleased to find two kilted pipers wearing Black Watch tartan playing in the streets. When I hailed them as Scotsmen they answered me in the accents of Cork! 'It's Irish we are entirely,' they said. 'Would ye care to subscribe some little thing, now, to the pipe band of Cark?'

H. V. Morton, *In Search of Ireland*, 1930

Catherine de Courcy

Coincidence, if there is such a thing, is always interesting to a travel writer. This coincidence starts in Papua New Guinea in 1986, travels through the Australian outback, into the depths of grief, back to Ireland and includes fishing on the Blackwater and memorable nights in the Ballyrafter House Hotel in Lismore. On the way it takes in Vietnam, the Golden Triangle, Phuket and Dubai. In 2009, when Mary Houlihan invited me to speak at Immrama about *An adventure in grief*, I had no idea that there was a coincidence waiting for me in Lismore.

I first attended Immrama in 2004 and enjoyed the travel-related conversations that took place over the weekend. On Sunday morning, over a big Irish breakfast in Ballyrafter House, Paul Clements led a lively discussion about responsibility of writers towards people they meet. Having chatted with him in the Rustic Café the previous day, Paul involved me when the discussion turned to Australia. I had just returned to Ireland after 18 years abroad, two of which were in Papua New Guinea and the remainder in Australia. My husband, John Johnson, and I had written two Australian desert travel books. In 2005 I was invited to conduct the Immrama writing workshop and to introduce Michael Palin to a large audience. Once again travel chat started on the Friday evening, this time after Brian Keenan's magical talk about Alaska, continued through a warm Saturday evening on benches overlooking the Ballyrafter Hotel gardens and finally ended on Sunday after breakfast with Dick Warner.

Early in 2009 I published *An adventure in grief*, a memoir and exploration of grief following my husband's suicide. Although it contained a lot of personal information, I considered it a travel book. The eight years since John's death in December 2000 had involved plenty of geographical travel, including my return to Ireland in 2003. However the focus of the book was the weird and wonderful adventure into my spiritual self. I had had spiritual experiences on my travels, such as in Buddhist temples in the Golden Triangle or observing the spiritual cleaning of the streets in Phuket. In Australia, when I was in the silent and beautiful desert, I often felt like I was absorbing a tonic that calmed the soul. Even when John was being consumed by post-traumatic stress from his military service in Vietnam in 1968-9, the desert was the one place where he could find peace. Yet, prior to John's death, my sense of spirit was firmly sceptical.

The morning after John died, I spoke on the phone to a woman in Ireland named Maria who, with only John's name to go on, told me about the lead up to his death. I was too shocked by the events of the previous evening to wonder how she could have been so accurate in an apparent information vacuum and simply accepted what she had said. As she spoke, I suddenly saw life and death as a continuum separated only by a mindset and I could understand John's decision to die in the context of that continuum. This gave me a perspective that brought peace, despite physical exhaustion and deep distress. From my own cultural perspective, it was unorthodox and perhaps a little dangerous for my long-term mental health. But travel experiences, which had pushed me outside my comfort zone and allowed me to glimpse different ways in which people viewed the world, demanded that I see where this approach would lead.

As my adventure into the strange world of alternative worldviews continued, I began to enjoy it. By 2009, when I was introduced by Edward Lynch before an audience in the Courthouse Theatre at Immrama, it felt good to be alive once more. The weekend spent in conversation with Manchán Magan, Dermot Somers, Catherine Rotte-Murray and Gerdette Rooney, a traveller and regular visitor to the festival, was great fun.

Along with the other speakers, I stayed at the Ballyrafter Hotel in 2005 and 2009, but it was only in 2011 that I learnt of the Lismore coincidence. In 1986, an English friend called Jason Peers had introduced me to my future husband, John Johnson, in Papua New Guinea. In 1995, Jason, who was then living in Dubai, came to Ireland to take John on a stag week around the country prior to our marriage in Dublin. Over the years, I had heard stories about this week from both John and Jason. A lengthy story about fishing somewhere in Waterford and a dinner in a local hotel had been repeated often but I had not listened attentively to the detail. Then one sunny lunchtime in September 2011, I received a call from Jason, who was on a nostalgia trip around Ireland with his son. The Waterford hotel from the stag week was on their itinerary. It emerged that John and Jason had stayed in the Ballyrafter and Noreen Willoughby remembered them both. Before long, she made the connection with me and Jason rang to tell me this.

The Blue Sky Bends Over All

It was lovely that John and I had spent a night in the same hotel ten years, and then 14 years apart. The excitement of this coincidence had much to do with the importance of Immrama to me as a professional writer: after a successful publishing career abroad, it takes time to establish oneself in another country. From that first Immrama weekend when Paul Clements drew me into the discussion, I have always thought of Lismore as the place that welcomed me back to Ireland as a writer. Coincidence or not, who knows? But I really like the idea that John was connected to this aspect of my continuing life.

The next excitement was the sight of the sea at Dungarvan, rather like Woolacombe Bay, a combe with streams and a cove at the foot of it. There was also a ruined Abbey. Behind on the landward side rose the Knockmealdown Mountains. Dungarvan is quite a sizeable place with sand dune, a wide estuary and plenty of houses. A honeymoon couple were being seen off by a large crowd of ill-dressed friends and relatives. At Cappagh, I saw another milk-factory and a notice that the Cork City otter-hounds would meet on Sunday. We came to a mass of thatched white cottages and crossed the Blackwater at Cappoquin. The Blackwater is a wide, black and famous salmon river which has lately been acquired by the Duke of Devonshire. At Clandalane, I saw a church in ruins and some very active flour mills not in ruins. The Blackwater valley is well wooded and fertile, and bears a look of North Devon. At Lismore, where the Duke of Devonshire has a house, we fed again on a mixed grill and whisky.

S. P. B. Mais, *I Return to Ireland*, 1948

Manchán Magan

The Immrama Festival of Travel Writing is the armchair traveller's Superbowl, our Kumbh Mela, our Eucharistic Congress. Each year a call arises from deep within us to congregate in the fairytale town of Lismore, to pay homage to our heroes, the pantheon of travel writing deities that the Immrama Festival manages to bring together. In the past, we've got to meet: Nick Danziger, Redmond O'Hanlon, Tim Butcher and Michael Palin.

I remember how my brain buzzed for days from the thrill of receiving benediction from the great philosopher/travel-writer, Pico Iyer, at Lismore Courthouse Theatre in 2010. Iyer represents the pinnacle of travel writer as sage, prophet and parable-weaver extraordinaire; to have him address us in a humble market town in Munster was a highlight of my year. The day after his talk, Sir Ranulph Fiennes shared his coldly heroic outlook on the world in the gym hall of the local school, and that night there was an audience with Tim Severin. The following evening, the uncrowned queen of travel writing, Jan Morris, read to us in the sumptuous surroundings of Fort William House – for those of us who dare follow in her footsteps, the subtly and incisiveness of Morris' prose acts as both carrot and stick.

Part of the success of Immrama as a boutique literary festival is that the people of Lismore are so supportive of it. The welcome that we, nomadic monkeys-with-typewriters, receive over these blissful June days is something to savour. Their appreciation of us and our much maligned craft (is art-form too ostentatious?) is rare and precious. Of course, they were blessed with an early introduction to good travel writing from their most famous citizen, Dervla Murphy, and it seems that this early immersion has honed their critical faculty.

The Blue Sky Bends Over All

They've come to understand what we already know, that travel writers are invariably better yarn spinners than most writers. The open road hones one's inner seanchaí; the long sojourns alone temper the profundity of one's insights. Any group of travellers around an open fire or gathered in some seedy flophouse will invariably start telling tales, and unless you can hold your own, you're soon eclipsed. We've all started out being the quiet dull one sitting on our bunk alone, and worked our way up through the ranks, so that we can hold a dorm or a campsite of weary wanderers under our spell – or, even the notoriously discerning breakfast audience at the Immrama Literary Breakfast. This particular crowd of hungry, erudite armchair travellers from Lismore, Dungarvan and Cappoquin are far more demanding than any typical bunch of weary backpackers who may only half-listen as they pick away at their blisters, mend their rucksacks and slurp noodles from battered pots.

Although Dervla Murphy does not generally make an appearance at Immrama her influence on the festival cannot be overemphasized. She is Ireland's most extraordinary and intrepid voyager since Saint Brendan, and without doubt the beating heart of Immrama. One of the greatest attractions for any travel writer visiting Lismore is the vague chance that we might catch a glimpse of our heroine as she scurries down to the Blackwater for a swim or to bring the dogs for a dawn walk. Dervla was the lodestar for all of us in Ireland who dreamt of exploring the world. She made it seem so easy. Am I in safe enough company here to admit that I had a crush on her for years?

The potential of possibly catching a glimpse of her emerging from or retreating back into her appropriately medieval Irish *caravansari* tucked behind the main street still adds an extra frisson to every visit to the town. Before I ever met her I used to dream of coming across her, seeing her riding over the bleak Afghani wasteland towards me on her trusty old bike. I'd frantically try to think of something devastatingly clever to say that would make her dismount and join me by the campfire so that we could talk and share ideas into the night.

We all, I suppose, dream of getting to stay in Dervla's timeless warren, and such is the depth of her hospitality that if she could she would extend an invitation to all, but she tends to be abroad at festival time and, in any event, there are so many other fine places to stay in town. Lismore House Hotel is always the centre of Immrama festivities and is ideally located on the main street. For the ultimate blow-out, one could revel in the luxury of Lismore Castle for €3,500 per night, or, if that seems steep, a room at the castle's old dowager house, Ballyrafter House Hotel, can be had for 2% of the cost of the castle. The owner Joe Willoughby hosts many of the travel writers, and over the years I've seen Fergal Keane, Rory MacLean and Jan Morris all enjoying the unassuming, comfortable-in-its-skin gentility of the place. Michael Palin has made positive comments about the views of the floodlit towers and turrets at night across the Blackwater River, while Redmond O'Hanlon, the adventurer and author of *Into the Heart of Borneo,* revealed a penchant for the residents' lounge. On my last visit, Sir Ranulph Fiennes was purring like a cat in the conservatory.

It has to be said that no writer, no matter how great, could match the true highlight of any journey to Lismore in early summer – the rich mantle of rhododendron that covers the mountains in an alien, eye-popping display of hand-knotted purple carpet. It is on a whole other plane, dazzling and disorientating the mind. It's *Day of the Triffids* territory – an intensity of colour and texture that is disturbing – as if the area's famous witch, Petticoat Loose, has unloosed her eponymous garment. It is one of life's great synchronicities that Immrama is held at the precise moment that these crimson jewels are in full bloom. Perhaps nature and literature are vying with each other, but for me, they coalesce perfectly. When I am driving up and over the Knockmealdown Mountains twisting back and forth along the hairpin bends and through the Vee surrounded by this blanket of beauty, knowing that three days of travel writing treats lie ahead, I am truly happy.

Immrama at 10 years of age is really only now getting into its stride. As a rare haven where travel writing is respected it has a pivotal role to play. While too often travel writers are dismissed as literature's tiramisu – fluffy, soaked in booze and of little sustenance – Lismore allows us the chance to show our true colours. The festival recognizes the overlooked fact that travel writing is the only art form that has as its aim to celebrate the world, to bridge cultures and break down barriers. If, as a race, we are to have any chance of survival then we are going to have to get to know each other, to accept that beyond our differences we are one. Travel writers and their readers are more aware of this fact than any, and, as such, have a duty to continue spreading the gospel, converting people, *duine i ndiaidh duine,* (person by person) from the narrowness of tribalism, nationalism and parochialism to a new more open appreciation of the wonders of our shared world.

Immrama can be at the very heart of this; not just celebrating the past heroics of old frozen-bearded fogies, but finding and championing fresh perspectives and new formats through which we can explore our world.

Go fada buan sibh, Immrama!

Quite recently the Irish Government had taken over the netting rights of all salmon in every river and lake in the Twenty-six Counties. I do not know what compensation was paid to the Duke of Devonshire, but before the war the fishing rights were worth several thousands of pounds a year. Monks had devised a killing hatch quite close to the castle and it was still in operation several hundreds of years later. It consisted of wooden piles built into a side channel to attract any unwary salmon which did not go straight up the stream. All that you had to do was to lower the net, pull up dozens of beautiful twenty-and thirty-pounders with the sea lice still on their tails, and then bang them on the head with a club – not every sporting, but most lucrative. Poaching on the Blackwater was very prevalent in the 'thirties, and I shall never forget one afternoon when I went out with my host, his water bailiff, a rifle, a shotgun, and revolver to look for poachers' nets. We received many black looks from the bank, but found nothing on this occasion. On previous expeditions of this sort, a couple of nets had been discovered and removed. One of them was used to protect the strawberries in the grounds of the castle, much to the annoyance of the poachers to whom it had belonged and who asked for its return. The reason for carrying the rifle, shotgun, and revolver was quite simple. Members of the previous house-parties had been shot at more than once in the past.

Charles Graves, *Ireland Revisited*, 1949

Hadani Ditmars

"In the desert of life, the wise person travels by caravan, while the fool prefers to travel alone." – Arabic proverb

"There is a distant isle / Around which sea horses glisten… / Begin a voyage across the clear sea" – the words with which an unknown "vision woman" lures Bran to travel, from *The Voyage of Bran*

The mystery of travel remains elusive. Why do some of us feel compelled to wander, while others are content to stay at home? And why do some of us feel the urge to write about our journeys? Worthy questions to contemplate over a glass of Guinness at Immrama Lismore – Festival of Travel Writing – one of my favourite literary destinations.

When I was invited to read from my book *Dancing in the No Fly Zone* in 2006, in keeping with that year's festival theme "Travel and Conflict", I became enchanted by Lismore. I learned that it had been a centre of learning since its mystical origins in the seventh century, when a local "wise woman" was said to have welcomed St. Carthage with a prophecy that he would found *lios more*, or "big fort."

In 1171, Norman King Henry II of England built a castle on the former monastic site; according to many accounts, the Irish clergy colluded with the English monarch to advance their own agenda. Now, Henry's castle, rebuilt in the 19th century, belongs to the Duke of Devonshire, and his son, Lord Burlington, has opened a cutting-edge art gallery inside – a delightful discovery.

A highlight of my visit was with a group of old-timers playing gorgeous fiddle music and traditional Irish tunes at The Classroom pub in downtown Lismore (all 500 metres of it). They graciously let me sing *She Moved through the Fair,* and didn't bat an eye when I sang *The Next Market Day*, with a certain Canadian naïveté, not realizing it was a song from the North.

I reflected then on how Ireland's deadly identity politics had been trumped by the country's recent economic boom and lively arts scene. And yet, in a country that has seen its fair share of hard times, there was such an innate understanding of Iraq, and its sectarian strife, resistance to occupation and spirit of cultural defiance, that my book struck a deeply resonant chord. From the land of 1001 nights to the Emerald Isle, there was an unbroken chain of stories – men and women who loved their homeland, but were often compelled to leave it, and travel to distant lands. It was the stories of Iraqis- whose narratives were being ignored, and whose very culture was being erased – that had drawn me back to Baghdad so many times. And now, in Lismore, I was being drawn into the Irish story.

At a round table discussion on Ireland and the Middle East, I spoke of peace and conflict with Brid Rogers, and a group that included RTE correspondent Charlie Bird and journalist Margaret Ward, and found many natural connections.

Ireland is a land with which I have only recently developed a romance. And yet I feel an odd but undeniable resonance with the Middle East. Not just in terms of tribalism and sectarian conflict, but also in terms of the story telling and poetic traditions that are so important in both places. (*Immrama* – from the old Irish word for journey – made me think of *Inanna* – the Sumerian goddess of love, war and fertility who travelled to the underworld and back).

In 2006, the Irish – who themselves were traditionally economic migrants – were dealing with their new found boom-induced influx of international workers, many from the Arab and Muslim world – and the time seemed ripe for inter-cultural dialogue. As I would discover, Galway-based writer Bob Quinn, whose book *The Atlantean Irish* is a fascinating read, makes an argument for a direct cultural, musical, mythological and linguistic connection between Irish and Arab culture – via maritime medieval trade routes.

As I spent my days in Lismore, meeting with fellow festival participants – including Irish poet Louis de Paor and storyteller/actor Nuala Hayes – and the evenings in the local pubs where everyone broke into spontaneous song and storytelling, I began to lose myself in the spirit of the place.

Lismore revealed itself as a place full of fantastic tales: farmers who guard against the evil eye that would render their fields infertile, night creatures from the Blackwater River, benevolent fairies and mischievous pookas (these stories were not foreign to me, having worked in lands where tales of *djinn*, "genies", were part of the cultural norm.) It was a place that seemed real enough and yet might disappear into the mist at any moment. Combined with the fact that I seemed to be in a strange, no mobile phone reception zone, my five days in Lismore seemed like five centuries, and yet passed in the blink of an eye.

The highlight of the entire Lismore experience was undoubtedly the last night at The Classroom pub, when a spontaneous, Guinness-assisted performance took place. De Paor recited poetry in Irish and English, I sang some Russian gypsy songs (much to the delight of a man from Odessa, newly-wed to the Irish barmaid), and Hayes told her wonderful rendition of the story of Bran, which she says is really about the dawn of the travel tale.

As she recounted the story of the mythical islands to the west, of the magical Land of Women, where Bran was lured by promises of eternal bliss, of great feasts and luxurious seaweed baths, of fruit hanging heavy on trees, she reawakened in me the wonder of travel. And as she told of Bran's turning to dust upon his return home and the recording of his journeys on tablets of stone, I remembered again why I felt so compelled to write it all down.

Lismore is a beautiful old town into which all the gentleness of the country about it seems to have seeped. The bedroom of the hotel where we stayed was decorated with a set of "The Drunkard's Progress": "The Expectant Mother," "Sick with Remorse," "The Relapse." The staircase was decorated with scenes from the Crimea War. One could produce a wonderful exhibition of pictures from Irish country hotels. There is a cathedral of sorts, a seventeenth-century successor of a whole series of churches from the sixth century onwards, of which little now remains. Lismore seems to have been the capital of the Irish Reformation of the twelfth century…The Catholic cathedral in the well-known Cork blend of limestone and purple sandstone is a sorry affair, but the tree-lined streets and Georgian houses against their background of pale mountain are lovely.

Frank O'Connor, *Leinster, Munster & Connaught*, 1950

Michael Shapiro

"Trying to interview Dervla Murphy is like trying to open an oyster...with a wet bus ticket."

That line came from the 2010 documentary 'Who is Dervla Murphy?' about the intrepid Irish travel writer. In 2003, I'd hoped to go to Ireland to interview the author of *Full Tilt* and *Eight Feet in the Andes* for my book *A Sense of Place*, a collection of conversations with the world's leading travel writers. But each time I went overseas to conduct interviews for the book, Dervla was on the road.

Then something serendipitous happened. The organizers of Immrama contacted me asking if I could put them in touch with Jonathan Raban, who appears in *A Sense of Place*. I said sure and asked where the festival is.

"Lismore in County Waterford," said Mary Houlihan, the vivacious organizer of the festival, "down in the south of Ireland," she added graciously, in case I didn't know.

"Lismore," I rolled the name through my mind and then it clicked. "Isn't that where Dervla Murphy lives?"

"Indeed it is," Mary said.

Before she finished that short sentence I was mentally booking my airline ticket. "So Dervla will be headlining the festival?" I asked.

"Well," said Mary, "She's not much for publicity. She usually disappears during Immrama. But we have some other fine writers this year. Jan Morris and Pico Iyer are coming, and so is Sir Ranulph Fiennes."

I almost fell out of my chair: two of the world's most accomplished authors about place joined by the polar explorer who crossed the length of Antarctica by foot and ran seven marathons in seven days on seven continents. Fiennes was the first person to reach the North and South Pole overland, but here's what I remember about him: he pulled a sled from icy waters during an attempt to walk solo to the North Pole in 2000 and suffered from frostbite on his hands. On his return to Britain, he found the pain untenable and, unwilling to wait for a doctor, took a Black & Decker to his fingers to cut off the dead tips.

"Maybe you could find a way here," Mary said, explaining that Lismore offered more than just the festival. And she hooked me with a passing remark: the Celtic Tiger never quite made it to West Waterford. The pubs, inns and landscape have remained virtually untouched by the whirlwind of prosperity that had whipped through Ireland transforming Dublin and other Irish cities before disappearing in a deluge of debt.

The timing of the festival was perfect: I could combine a visit to Dublin for Bloomsday, held every 16 June when just about everyone in the city dresses up as characters from James Joyce's *Ulysses*, with a trip to Lismore for Immrama. I booked tickets for myself and my girlfriend, Jackie.

Two months later I'm in Dervla Murphy's garden, hoisting a couple of frothy pints, her three little dogs climbing all over us. It's true, Dervla rarely does interviews these days, but not because she's aloof or introverted; she's about as far from pretentious as you can get. "It's just that I hate people fizzing about me," she says in her booming Irish brogue, explaining her plan to leave for Dublin the next morning and skip Immrama.

She's wearing a light blue jacket over a navy sweater with a button that says "No War." Her dog, Wurzel, has shed all over Dervla's dark pants but she doesn't care. Just over a year shy of her 80th birthday, when I interviewed her in June 2010, she appears fit and strong enough to ride her bike from Ireland to India, which she'd done almost a half century before as chronicled in *Full Tilt*.

Many travel writers end up settling far from home, such as British author Pico Iyer who lives in Japan. Others, such as Jan Morris of Wales, are so deeply of their place it's hard to imagine them living anywhere else. Dervla, as everyone in town calls her, belongs in – and to – Ireland.

"I've seen so many really magnificent landscapes in so many different countries, but I suppose I just feel I belong here," she said. "There have been so many changes in Ireland, many changes for the worse during the last 15 or 20 years, with quite unnecessary motorways here, there and everywhere, but this little corner of West Waterford is almost unchanged. It's a feeling for the landscape really, I can't imagine living anywhere else."

After travelling over rhododendron-blanketed green hills with their gentle streams and graceful trees to reach Lismore, I understand why Dervla feels so at home here. We talk about travel, writing, and her remarkable life: how, at the age of 10, she sat on Round Hill, just over a mile from where we're speaking, and vowed to pedal a bike to India; about how she took her tea from a mug at a time when ladies used a cup and saucer, her penchant for blue jeans, her decision to have a child out of wedlock at a time when that just wasn't done.

The interview complete, I get Jackie at our hotel and Dervla gives us a tour of her house, The Old Market, a collection of stone buildings surrounding a courtyard that served as Lismore's marketplace for centuries. The market closed in 1909 and had fallen into disrepair. Dervla bought it in the late 1970s and found it "in complete ruin, no roof and rubble piled up inside, earth and weeds growing out of the wall." She shows me rusted wagon wheels that were left behind, an ancient scale and other decaying remnants from the market's past.

In her study, which dates to the late seventeenth century, is a typewriter – not a computer – which she uses to compose her books. It's covered by a Tibetan flag. She's too humble to mention it, but later I learn the flag was a gift from the Dalai Lama. The guest room, where Michael Palin stayed while in Lismore, was once the market's "piggery."

Dervla lovingly shows us her vast collection of books, including volumes that belonged to her grandfather. Then she picks up a greeting card someone sent her with the words: "Beer is proof that God loves us… and wants us to be happy."

The next day Mary Houlihan takes time out to show Jackie and me a slice of County Waterford. The highlight is Ardmore, believed to be the oldest Christian settlement in Ireland, dating to the fourth century. We saunter among the tombstones and ruins of St. Declan's church and gaze up at a round stone tower, almost 100 feet tall, that dates to the twelfth century and was used to keep prized possessions out of the hands of marauding Vikings.

We walk a short segment of St Declan's Way, an old pilgrimage route that goes from Ardmore to Lismore and on to the Rock of Cashel in County Tipperary. We're enthralled by rolling emerald hills and sea views, but by foot it would be a long way to Tipperary. We opt for lunch at the Cliff House Hotel, which has a Michelin-star restaurant overlooking Ardmore Bay. The misty views make me want to recite a poem by Yeats, or break out into a Van Morrison song.

On the way back to Lismore, we stop into a shop to meet Bernard Leddy, the Mayor of Lismore. The bible was translated into Gaelic in Lismore, he says, noting that in the Middle Ages the village was one of Europe's top universities. Not only that, Marco Polo's life story was translated into Gaelic and found tucked away in the walls of Lismore Castle. And Walter Raleigh once took refuge in the castle. "The streams of history run very deep through Lismore," Leddy says.

That night Jackie and I head to The Classroom, a vintage Lismore pub. I order a Guinness and as I'm waiting for it to settle, local resident Eddie Hanley walks over and says to me: "A Guinness has to stand, and when a customer isn't a regular it has to stand longer." Then I meet an Irish Joe the Plumber who's also the postman and tells me he carries his tools with him, fixing leaky faucets as he walks his mail route.

The band that Thursday night is an assemblage of guitars, Irish (*Uilleann*) pipes and an accordion. When they play the national anthem everyone stops drinking – including the young blokes enjoying poker – and rises to their feet. The bar's owner, Willie Roche, says some visitors of Irish origin become so emotional hearing traditional music that it makes him cry. "We give them the venue to express themselves; life is about being happy," he says, pint in hand. "This is our culture. The government comes down so hard on you if you sell drink, but they should promote something like this, then you'll remember Ireland for what it's worth." A glimmer in his eye, he adds: "You know the definition of a gentleman? Someone who can play the pipes…but doesn't."

The next day Jackie and I join Pico Iyer and his wife Hiroko for a float down the Blackwater. We board a battered wooden boat "for a journey that goes back 300 or 400 years," says our poetic captain, Tony O'Gallagher. His first mate, a little dog called Pharaoh, hunkers down on top of the unused life vests. We float by majestic towers and tumbledown buildings as the sun and clouds play a game of hide-and-seek. "I love it – it's a privilege to find something like this," Tony says, relishing his job. "Better than fucking acting."

That night we're wowed by Iyer's talk, his observations stated so eloquently and rapidly that my mind races to stay with him. The next morning I awake to hear verses ringing out over the town square and floating through our open window. It's local poet Louis de Paor, who will later read to the accompaniment of Irish pipes, being broadcast for all to hear.

The rest of the festival is a whirlwind of serendipity. One night at dinner, Jackie and I end up at the same table as Jan Morris and her companion Elizabeth. On Sunday morning, we visit St. Carthage's Cathedral and hear the priest say: "He who sings, prays twice." How Irish. Morris closes the festival in conversation with Iyer and Paul Clements, editor of a collection of tributes to the Welsh author. It's everything one expects from Morris: witty, insightful, provocative, and most of all, fun.

Jackie and I have one more day left in Lismore. We tour Lismore castle and gardens, then stroll along Lady Louisa's Walk, which parallels the River Blackwater, verdant branches arching over our heads. Overcome by the magic of the place but thoroughly unprepared, I ask Jackie to sit with me on a riverside bench. She comments on the birds, the trees, the yellow and purple wildflowers. I don't have a diamond, but I do have a hematite ring, an iron band I'd bought a month before for 79 cents while on assignment in Alaska. Tears welling in my eyes, I ask. She says yes, yes, yes, as fervently as Molly Bloom at the end of *Ulysses.*

The Knockmealdowns are elongated east-west, but are a compact group of hills rather than a range. They are dark with heather, and cut by the deep gash of the V-road pass. From all angles they stand out a most symmetrical group, Knockmealdown itself a graceful cone with the subsidiary heights grouped about it. In detail they are humpy and fail to live up to the promise of the distant view; in reality a group of uplands commanding an outlook over all the plains around and with the church of the Cistercian abbey of Mount Melleray flashing white upon their flank. Yet the Knockmealdowns, if not exciting to the climber, have the virtue of never looking tame.

Daphne Pochin Mould, *The Mountains of Ireland*, 1955

Alan Murphy

As castles go, you'd be hard put to find a more sumptuous example than Lismore's own. Nestled in its lush greenery, its vista reminds visitors and returning locals alike that they have arrived somewhere a bit special. Should Hollywood come a-knocking with a medieval epic in mind, it might well find itself beholding the perfect bucolic pile: the original edifice upon which legends are based.

Stumbling into Lismore in 2008, I knew nothing about the place. I knew one person there – artist and writer Corina Duyn – who was waiting to help me with a children's book I was planning to publish. The name Dervla Murphy meant nothing to me (for shame!), and was there a festival that sometimes took place there? I hadn't even got the town's pronunciation right, for pity's sake. It amazes me now that it could ever have been so.

Somehow I ended up staying on and eventually, by coincidence, found myself living above the local bookshop, Blackwater Books, for two years. (The owner Kevin Murphy was my landlord. My arrival thus brought the total number of bookish Lismoreians called Murphy up to a cosy three.)

Eventually, much sooner than I could have anticipated, I was offered a council house, and have been there ever since. It's a kind of artists' colony where I live: there's me (I illustrate my own books and am also a painter), my next-door neighbour the ceramicist Jane Jermyn and…well, that's about it for the moment. Suffice to say though that the town and its environs does tend to attract arty types and doesn't look like I'll be budging for a while.

Before setting foot in Lismore my concept of travel writing veered more towards *The Hitchhiker's Guide to the Galaxy* than to Sir Ranulph Fiennes, and I still have a penchant for the more imaginative kind of journey. In this context I've managed to gatecrash Immrama three times as a "non-serious" poet. (My writing is more likely to involve rubbish-collecting aliens than evocations of Cuba). My physical travels have generally been confined by the boundaries of this island, though, since moving, I have developed my hitchhiking skills a little!

And I think it's fair to say also that I've prospered since coming here. Despite a long-term illness I've managed to publish two well received books and have given a whole host of public readings of my (rather skewed) poetry (which means that I spend a lot of time out of town). Having launched my first book in the town library in 2009 (as part of the festival that year), I was lucky enough to be asked to launch the second one, *Psychosilly,* alongside books by Áine Uí Fhoghlú, Paul Clements and David Monagan, as the inaugural event of the 2011 festival in Lismore Castle itself. It's not every day you get to plug a book in a castle.

That evening event was a bit of a whirlwind for me, and was notable for its odd occurrences: my normally sturdy mother was fainting in the heat and had to be brought out into the foyer, local artist Michael Mulcahy gave an impromptu (and rather deranged) speech at the end of the night, and as I, Eugene Dennis and a number of others trooped out afterwards, we chanced upon a strange immobile bird, perched as if stuffed on a rock in the castle grounds. We then repaired to Lismore House Hotel and later to Eamonn's pub for a few relieved drinks. The opening had been mobbed (as was Eamonn's) and boded well for the rest of the festival.

There's many a small Irish town that's not in danger of becoming overpopulated any time soon. In these places bleak winter clouds are often more numerous than conversations and the wind can be heard to whistle in the key of desolation. Cows and tumbleweeds help to make up the numbers. To be honest, Lismore doesn't entirely escape this fate but in the summer months it does generate a significant buzz, especially around the time of the festival. Tourists, from far and near, come and go. My brother, his partner and their two children stayed in Ballyrafter House during the 2009 festival and loved it. Their reaction is typical of visitors and Lismore certainly boasts some gobsmacking other locations in which it hosts its cultural events, such as Fort William House where Jan Morris gave a memorable talk in 2010.

Other memories: poet Christy Parker bringing the house down with his raucous verse, as MC in the increasingly popular open mic event in 2009; shooting the breeze with Lismore's young inhabitants in a poetry session that Pippa Sweeney also hosted, in the Millennium Park in 2010; showing my cousin the bicycle on the wall of Lismore library at my 2009 launch, and explaining that it was the very one that the "crazy woman" who cycled to India that he was talking about used, and that she lived in the town.

So thank you to Lismore for helping me to thrive and succeed. And thank you to the Immrama committee for having me these last few years. All involved should be justly proud of what they have achieved with the festival. Long may it continue.

There was hardly a drop of rain all the time and the whole castle and the primeval forest round it were spellbound in a late spring or early summer trance; heavy rhododendron blossom everywhere and, under the Rapunzel tower I inhabited, a still leafless magnolia tree shedding petals like giant snowflakes over the parallel stripes of an embattled new-mown lawn: silver fish flickered in the river, wood pigeons cooed and herons slowly wheeled through the trees so overgrown with lichen they looked like green coral, drooping with ferns and lianas, almost like an equatorial jungle. One would hardly have been surprised to see a pterodactyl or an archaeopteryx sail through the twilight, or the neck of a dinosaur craning through the ferns and lapping up a few bushels out of the Blackwater, which curls away like the Limpopo, all set about with fever-trees.

Letter from Patrick Leigh Fermor to Daphne and Xan Fielding, May 1956,
written at Lismore Castle and extracted from *In Tearing Haste,*
Letters between Deborah Devonshire and Patrick Leigh Fermor, 2008
Edited by Charlotte Mosley

Jan Morris

To my mind the best of memories are generally blurred – impressionistic memories, hazed, very likely inaccurate but indelible in the mind. Like Tolstoy's families, it seems to me, unhappy memories are sharp, individual and all too clear, but happy memories blend harmoniously one with another.

When, needing comfort for one reason or another, I turn to my own reservoir of experiences, I may summon lovely happenings in Venice, autumn evenings beside the Dwyfor at home, airport reunions, even good reviews, and often these glide easily enough into the few days I spent a year or two ago at the Immrama festival of travel literature at Lismore in County Waterford.

I don't exactly remember what happened. I forget who else was there. I've forgotten what Immrama means. But like the dapple of the waves at Venice, picking up conkers in Wales, meeting my beloved at Heathrow or rustling through the newspaper to find that kind critique, those few days at Lismore form part of my own happy family of recollection.

Of course it is partly just Ireland. It is always a marvel to me to find that Ireland is still there, still green, still merry, through all the buffetings of recent history. I don't like Dublin as much as I used to, I am repelled sometimes by the excrescences of the late Celtic Tiger and I wish the Irish bourgeoisie had never discovered the motor-car, but still whenever my ferry sails in past Howth Head, and I hear the thumps and rattles of our impending arrival at Dun Laoghaire, I feel a tingle of exuberance.

And Irishness at its most delightful vaguely dominates my memories of Immrama at Lismore. I recall the town as an Irish idyll itself, a homely handsome little place somewhere, with a fine old inn in its main street, and a castle above that belongs to an English duke, and a river with a handsome bridge, and all around, in and out of the town, all along the river, sweet, fresh and fragrant, the green trees of Ireland.

I remember it as a loitering place, easy but elegant, where we did our literary things against a background of fine old houses, to a cheerfully cultured audience, and I remember a farmers' market in the grounds of the Duke of Devonshire's castle, and dinner in a splendid hotel like a farmhouse just outside the town, and whiskey in a corner pub, where somebody told me, I'm almost sure, that Robert Boyle the philosopher was a Lismore man – Boyle of Boyle's Law. And wasn't there something about Fred Astaire – didn't his sister marry the Duke, or am I dreaming that too?

It's all a contented blur. This I do know for certain, though: that an American friend of mine, coming to the Immrama Festival that same year, and bewitched I suppose by the green and mellow seduction of Lismore, proposed to his inamorata down by the river, in the dapple of the trees, and now lives with her happily ever after in California.

Immrama. Oh yes, I remember its meaning now, I think. It's an old Celtic name for a class of poetry, rich in fable, tradition and ancient memory, which concerns voyaging to distant magical parts, such as the Land of Eternal Youth. And if I've got it right, Lismore is just the place for that travel writing festival – not quite *Tir na nOg* itself, perhaps, but one of the next best destinations.

A lovely castle it is, not quite worn out by being constantly looked at, and none the worse for being continually compared with the English castle of Warwick. It is also none the worse, in fact it is all the better, for the owner's refusal to admit the public. It is often better to want to see interiors than to see them....In the hotel I sat on a high stool in the bar beside a Lismore man, who was full of local lore. The late Duke was a good man who kept the Black and Tans out of Lismore. He used this room, where we are now drinking stout, as his office. "When I was a lad," said he of the other high stool, "the Duke would be in here writing and we used to gather outside that window after school and shout, 'How's the Dook?' He'd open the window then and throw us out sixpenny-bits. Of course we never missed a day asking how the Dook was.

Stephen Rynne, *All Ireland*, 1956

Damien Lewis

The road leading from the remote and windswept wilds of West Cork to the gently rolling green hills of Lismore felt for me like coming home. Hailing originally from Dorset, on the west coast of England, the wooded folds and close-cut valleys of Waterford reminded me so much of the playground of my childhood. And for my wife – who, together with our children I had dragged off to the ends of the earth when we'd gone to live near the fishing village of Schull – three thousand miles of an Atlantic Ocean, then next stop America – coming to Lismore was a rare chance to get a much-needed taste of civilization once again.

Lismore proved to be all we'd hoped for as we cruised through. We stopped at the castle, itself magnificent and breathtaking as it rose in crenellated folds above the lush green of the trees, its grand form reflected in the dark waters of the river that flows past the walls. We browsed the market stalls, brought some fine pasties for lunch, and whiled away half the afternoon there. The only trouble was that by the time we set off again we couldn't seem find the festival location itself. No matter who we asked, we kept getting given different instructions on how to get there – all very helpful but equally confusing – and I half-imagined myself ending up with that classic of West Cork road directions.

"Sure, if it's the festival you're wanting you shouldn't have started from here…"

But find Immrama we eventually did, the name of which hails from an old Irish saying meaning 'take to the oars' and reflecting the Irish people's long affinity with travel, and we fell in love immediately with its setting. A winding drive took us through verdant evening gardens, and brought us round to the front of a grand, but somehow homely feeling house. We were late by the time we arrived, and so we hurried inside with our cases, only to be met by that typically unhurried Irish welcome which always serves to put the traveller at ease. And joy-of-joys, with friends having taken our children for the weekend, my wife and I were free to have a rare romantic dinner in the fine but cozy dining room.

Typifying how Ireland draws such a varied international clientele of visitors, a grand table was arranged down the centre of the dining hall, and was heaving with dozens of high-spirited men of a clearly Nordic persuasion. They were wearing odd tweedy jackets and knee-length breeches, and what looked suspiciously like lederhosen. Inevitably we got chatting, and they turned out to be a group of Icelandic men who'd come to enjoy a week fly-fishing in the rivers of Waterford, seeking the fine trout that are to be had there.

By the end of the evening I was a little confused as to whether fishing or drinking was their favoured pastime; countless toasts had been had by all, ourselves included, at their behest and upon their boundless hospitality – and my wife and I had seen romance go rapidly out the window. Not a bother. That wasn't the main worry. It had been a wild and fine old evening. The real worry was that I had to be up with the larks the following morning, for I was presenting the literary breakfast to the Immrama audience – which, as it sounds, is a talk given by an author to those participating in the festival over breakfast. Several things follow. One, it starts early. Two, people can be very grumpy over their coffee, toast and cereal. And three, I was going to have a stinking hangover, or so I feared.

As it happens, my wife and I had been fed a good deal of Icelandic fire water, or it could have been Irish poteen; I really can't remember which and I rose feeling almost as right as rain. Yet my stomach was still a knot of nerves, and this had little to do with the over-indulgence of the previous evening. My talk was going to take the audience on a journey into the remote Nuba Mountains of Sudan. From there it would continue to that nation's Western Darfur deserts, onwards into Asia, and Burma, and from there back to Africa, and into the Africa's biggest slum in Kenya's capital, Nairobi, from where I had just recently told the story of the US President's half-brother, Barack Obama, who lives in that seething ghetto.

It was one extraordinary and wide-ranging tour upon which to take my audience, and some of the issues: slavery, human rights abuse, the poverty of the slums, didn't exactly strike me as being the kind of topic to quicken the appetite over breakfast. But that, of course, is where I had underestimated the Immrama audience arranged before me. To call them well-travelled, cultured and with an eye to the more off-the-beaten-track parts of the world – and the issues that so often go with those areas – is an understatement. I have rarely, if ever, spoken for an hour over such wide-ranging and challenging topics as I did that morning - all the while trying to find a clear path through a slightly post-alcoholic haze - and had such a spellbound or appreciative audience.

The Blue Sky Bends Over All

Having spoken about a modern-day Nuba princess captured and sold as a slave, a Burmese girl who had to flee her homeland under vicious attack, a woman's epic trek out of the horror and darkness of Darfur, and the US President's half-brother's struggles to bring development into Africa's biggest slum, I decided to end on a high, or perhaps rather a lighter note. I spoke last of a book that I had just finished writing, one which was a complete departure from normal. I had just completed *Up Kilimanjaro*, a humorous travel book following myself and a fellow English friend living in Ireland, as we attempted to scale Africa's highest mountain, Kilimanjaro, where snowcaps glisten on the very equator.

What you might ask is amusing about climbing a 19,000-foot mountain, one that over half those who attempt, fail to summit and which claims many lives a year due to altitude sickness? Well, it had been very, very funny for me. I'd laughed my way up the mountain. And I had done so because my travelling companion Jimmy Gale was an overweight forty-something dog food salesman who'd rarely travelled outside the British Isles, let alone into deepest darkest Africa. I talked about the book being something akin to Bill Bryson's *A Walk in theWoods* meets *The Hangover*, which the audience did indeed seem to find hilarious. As I described Mr. Gale's balding, breathless efforts to scale the magnificent mountain, with all the while his mobile phone kept trilling as customers phoned in another order of dog food (I kid you not; his Irish mobile actually worked on Africa's highest mountain – or at least it did until I sabotaged it) – people were in stitches.

I hadn't wanted to leave my audience with a bad taste after breakfast, and it did lift the talk and give my audience cause to smile. After a spirited question and answer session, I was signing some books and a reporter from the *Cork Echo* approached. We sat to one side and she did a long interview. Oddly, she seemed most taken by the Kilimanjaro story. She described it as my "Most outlandish manuscript yet, a poignant yet hilarious tale about climbing Kilimanjaro with a west cork dog food salesman. It was like Bill Bryson with attitude," she added. Well, there you have it. I couldn't have said it better myself. I joked about how my wife and I had got lost trying to find Immrama, but somehow Jimmy Gale and I had made it up that majestic mountain.

The gods must have been shining upon us, she said, or perhaps Jimmy Gale and I had gone to Africa with the blessings of countless Irish travellers at our backs – all those who had passed this way before us; which just goes to show, there's no point setting out on your travels unless you do so from the right departure point in the first place. Or as a West Cork resident might say: "Sure, if it's there you want to be getting to, boy, you shouldn't have started from here at all…"

South of Clonmel lie irresistible lands and shores that run between Waterford and Cork. In my childhood the Blackwater Valley, from Lismore by Cappoquin to Fermoy and on from there the magic railway trip to Cork, all that was known to me, and its richness – voluptuous overflow of smell and light and sound, of fruit too greedily eaten, of laughs that hardly stopped with sleep, of overcrowded, passionate, summer extravagance, of pony traps and boats and apple trees and apple-pie beds: 'Down the Inches' and 'Down Barnane', up to holy Melleray, out to Castlehyde to gather plums: *The Perils of Pauline* at The Assembly Rooms, tea with Miss Quinlan in The Square, Clarnico caramels at O'Keefe's: the train to Cork for 'The Arcadians'; and pony-drives to Watergrass Hill, and home by Ballyhooly for lemonade. This was the only drinkable lemonade in Ireland, Uncle Willy said. And we conceded he was right. (You hurt your thumb terribly if you pressed down the little glass ball in the neck of the bottle). Men wading with rods under the bridge at Fermoy, salmon like swords in the light, white monks hacking at pine-trees. A smell of summer – all things in excess – and the Blackwater foaming black.

Kate O'Brien, *My Ireland*, 1962

Annie G. Rogers

If the Old Irish origin of 'Immram' comes from 'rowing about' – then even more fundamental than writing about travel writing itself is a kind of play with the oars of words. Seeing where words might take us is the first kind of travel a writer encounters. I am not a travel writer, but I travel to Lismore, and when I get here, I write.

I am constantly going back and forth over the Atlantic from Massachusetts to this place of great beauty, winter and summer, as though I were some migrating bird. I am an outsider to Lismore. My voice does not carry its accents, history, humour, lineage, geography, or local character. People sometimes ask if I am enjoying my holiday here. I come on a three-month visitor's visa, collecting a lot of stamps on my American passport. When I'm in Lismore, I write and I paint.

Sometimes, I also join the Immrama Festival. Coming to writing in relation to Immrama has a history within the town. I woke up one morning in June 2002 in Lismore and realized that I was a stranger and longed for a small way to belong. This was the start of the Railway Station Writers Group that met with me each summer weekly for years on end in the old railway station waiting room, opened up generously by Caitriona MacReynolds and John O'Neill. I had taught writing workshops in the U.S., and I transposed some of the writing exercises and invented new ones for our group. I remember the long summer evenings, sun streaming in the tall windows, small tables cobbled together to make one large table, and heads bent, writing. We broke for tea and biscuits, lit lamps, and then read aloud. I was astonished at the individual signature in each voice and the power of the stories read each time we met.

I also met with a group of elders in Mitchelstown, though not so often and not for years on end. Aengus Carroll helped me to edit a small book of stories written by those two groups, *Charlie's Chasing the Sheep*, taking its title from Lismore native, Helen Leddy's very funny short story. James Hyde of Lismore Books published it and helped us to distribute it. When the Immrama committee asked me to write with people as part of the festival, it seemed an outgrowth of these local experiences, albeit with a larger group. All these activities gave me a sense of belonging in Lismore.

Writing is itself a journey, a passage through vastness that makes even the ordinary strange and new to us, even the familiar a bit unfamiliar. This journey with words creates a world of experience for writers and readers that does not exist outside of those words. And yet, between the lines, there are many things language can't carry. Like grace notes in music, or ghosts of unspoken thoughts, these are experiences still asking for words.

At this edge, the only form of writing that works for me is poetry. I was thrilled when the Immrama committee asked me to join the Irish poet Mary Branley to offer writing workshops, my second invitation to be part of the festival. Poetry, more than any other genre of writing carries what can't be summed up or translated into another form – a magical mix of language and music that registers in the body. Mary and I had wonderful sessions with small groups of writers, and their writings carried something amazing that had never been said before, and their voices were, yes, musical.

Throughout these connections with Immrama I have to remind myself that I am not, in fact, a travel writer. Writing travels through me, like a great oar stirring the water, and leaves what I write as the trace of a new experience. I love bringing others on this journey with me and I am delighted to be part of this tenth anniversary celebration. As I plan to retire in Lismore, I trust that the town will become more and more a settled home. Whatever part I have to play here, I hope it will include writing and writers.

This is a place of ancient renown and at the same time one of the prettiest and best kept towns in the whole of Ireland. Its ecclesiastical associations go back to the very early days of Christianity and the bishopric is ascribed to Saint Carthach, who flourished in the seventh century and whose establishment soon attracted not only learned and pious men from all over Europe but others of less peaceful tendencies, such as Danes and Ossorians, who burnt and looted the town and abbey many times...Lismore is indeed a beautiful place set in countryside of surpassing loveliness and I felt strongly about it, that spirit which seems only to abide in a community that enjoys the gracious benefit of what we knew in happier days as *the Big House*. The senseless destruction, in both our *uncivil* and *civil* wars of the early part of this century, of so many of our *Big Houses* is something of dire national loss that few of our more fanatical patriots have so far had the wisdom to understand.

Richard Hayward, *Munster and the City of Cork*, 1964

Jasper Winn

"The journey of a thousand miles begins with a single step." So goes the ancient Chinese – or maybe it's Arabic, or perhaps Malay, or Masai or it might even be Irish, or possibly it's everyone's – truism. It's the happy cliché reached for so oft by travel writers starting a piece about travelling. Well, similarly, the story of a thousand words begins with a single letter, which, in this case, seems to be 'T'.

Getting to Lismore for the 2011 Immrama Festival of Travel Writing doesn't actually entail a journey of a thousand miles. It's more like a hundred and fifty miles from Dublin. My first step, from Harold's Cross, points me in the direction of Bus Aras. There'll be a bus to Clommel or to Caher? Well, there's definitely one heading towards Cork, anyway, and I can hop out en route, right next to Lismore in, say – I checked a map – Fermoy. There's bound to be a small country bus scuttling its way to Lismore from there, I reassured myself.

On the bus I looked out of the window. Made a few notes for my talk. But mostly looked blankly at the new 'smart' phone in my hand, and randomly swiped and prodded its touch screen hoping to understand, and even control, its functions. This exemplar of modern communications – like the typewriter, and then the fax machine, followed by the internet and email and Facebook and now Twitter – was going to take me one step further away from the pure simplicity of the traveller with pen and paper (an ink-driven Waterman Hemisphere sits in my shirt pocket tucked next to a Muji notebook), and one step closer to continually being 'in the office.'

In theory getting emails and having the internet on the move means we're all even freer to travel the remoter corners of the world whilst still working. But deep down I doubt that it's going to bring much liberty. Rather the opposite. On my first long-distance trip in hitched trucks across the Sahara, and then on through West Africa pedalling a Flying Pigeon bike bought in the market in Ougadougou I was away from Ireland for five months.

In that time I made a single three-minute phone call home and sent and received a few – very few – letters via poste restante. That was freedom.

And this phone isn't even that smart – more an idiot savant technology; the kind of intelligence that can draw the skyline of Paris with every window and roof in the correct place but can't tie its shoelaces. It presumably does some things really well. But I'm having trouble making it do even those things. I did some more prodding. More swiping. More jabbing at likely looking icons. I'm trying to send a message. And check my emails. And above all put up a Tweet on Twitter. *I'm on a #bus, going to Lismore Travel Writing Festival #Immrama*, seems a fairly simple sentiment to broadcast to the world. The kind of thing that one would write if one had a smart-ish phone. But Twitter is not tweeting for me.

After a few decades of making my way around the world on long walks, or in kayaks, or by buying horses and riding off for a month or two, or pedalling across whole countries on secondhand single-speed bikes, I've come to define myself as a 'slow adventurer.' That's 'slow' as in 'slow food,' 'slow travel,' 'slow sex,' 'slow towns' and the rest of the 'slow' movement. The idea being that it's good to slow down and take one's time. Good to enjoy the journey and not fret about getting to the destination. Good to understand that the elements of randomness in being 'slow' are a reward not a punishment. Good are the chance meetings with people. And the things that happen that one could never have planned for because one didn't know that they existed before they happened. Slow adventures mean, above all, surprising, and being surprised by, oneself.

At Lismore I'm going to be talking about *Paddle; A long way around Ireland*, my book on a thousand mile sea-kayak circumnavigation of the Irish coastline. It was very much a slow adventure. Weather and sea conditions and my own ineptitude and random meetings and distractions made it not so much an expedition as an extended jaunt. There were strandings on deserted isles, paddling amongst breaching three tonne basking sharks, two weeks of shore leave in Dingle playing music whilst waiting for high winds to die down. I took two and a half months to do the first five hundred miles and only two and a half weeks to complete the last half thousand miles. But I'm not going to be just talking about *Paddle*. I'm part of – perhaps the only ingredient in – the Immrama Fringe. So, rather than just talking about travel I'm going to be taking people travelling and only then talking with them.

Denis Murray of Blackwater Boating is assembling a flotilla of canoes and kayaks and sit-on-tops, and some thirty of us are going to launch below Lismore Castle and paddle down through the tidal waters, and into creeks and through mazes of islands, past Cappoquin, under the viaduct and into the wider waters to reach Tourin House. Once ashore there'll be tea and cakes, and a slide show and a chat about my trip, and maybe a bit of music. The idea is that after our group of doughty seafarers have paddled their way the six or so miles down stream when they listen to my account of kayaking around Ireland they will be actually *know* the feel of water on a paddle blade, sense again the swing and the roll of the canoe under them, taste the salt in the air, recall the dip of a gulls' wing or the splash of a mullet. They'll be able to touch their damp clothing and stretch their aching muscles. Rather than merely hearing words about what it's like to paddle a kayak, the paddlers will have experienced the kayaking for themselves. That's the idea, anyway. It seems a good idea. Appropriate to Immrama, too.

The idea of an *immram* – setting off on a sea voyage just to see what might happen – seems the height of 'slow adventure.' *Immrama* always carried the possibility that one might not come back from one's journey.

In my case it was looking like that I might not get to Lismore in the first place. In Fermoy I was told, with comic timing, that I'd just missed the bus to Lismore…. 'by two years…it was taken out of service a few years back.' I stood on a back road and stuck my thumb out; an hour's wait and then a quick succession of lifts. A woman dropped me in a farm gateway. An elderly farmer picked me up and we made slow progress in his battered car as a tailback of traffic built behind us, and he pointed out interesting fields and told me who lived in which house and who'd died; a half-empty bottle of whiskey lay on the back seat. From the traffic forced to halt behind us as he stopped his car mid-road to drop me off and fumble out a slow handshake and blessings for the way lying before me, one driver amongst the many fuming with impatience beckoned me into her passenger seat. And dropped me on the edge of Lismore. I walked into town.

In a pocket my stupid-phone 'beeped.' And again. And then over and over. Twitter was on, now. And Facebook, too. Text messages were ribboning across the screen like ticker tape. And emails were clicking up.

The first message of note I received on the new phone – from a mutual acquaintance – was that Sir Patrick Leigh Fermor had died just hours before. Arguably the quintessential 'slow adventurer,' the master of pen-and-paper travel writing, and of long walks turned into inimitable prose, he was a man who had lived a long life to the full and enjoyed it all. And he was connected with Lismore too, joining those other traveller-writers – Spencer, Thackeray, Walter Raleigh, Dervla Murphy – also linked to the town.

Paddy's life added a poignant theme to the Immrama festival. It was recalled by Theo Dorgan and Sara Wheeler in their stage conversation, and again by William Blacker in his account of life in Romania as he told of meeting with him only a few months previously.

But *A Time of Gifts* and *Between the Woods and the Water,* and *A Time to Keep Silence* were also talked about in bars and cafés – though only amongst many other travel and writing subjects discussed.

Over the coming days I was to experience first-hand the Immrama magic. That, as in an Irish music *seisiún*, the speakers and audience are equally knowledgeable, and – once in a bar after the formal talks – they become interchangeable, with the telling of travel stories performed as if playing jigs and reels with all the ornamentation and invention necessary for rhythm and melody. I learnt, too, from an impassioned Bloggers Clinic that my fairly-smart phone was just part of the ongoing development in telling travellers' tales on a continuum from pre-historic fireside grunted anecdote to today's blogs and tweets and couch-surfing.

The famed breakfast talk, I discovered, was packed with people who, barely pre-dawn, seemed to display as much jollity and goodwill as they'd had only a few hours before when stretching 'last orders' into the early hours, and as much appetite for a full fry and strong coffee as they'd had for pints. And the Armada of small craft launches on the Sunday afternoon, and we make our way down the Blackwater, as I watch fascinated by the dynamics of the group, as some people coalesce into small bands of paddlers, whilst others break away, some people relishing the solitude, others the company, each on their own slow adventure.

Neither the journey of a thousand miles, nor that of a hundred and fifty, ends in a single footstep. There is no arrival point in travel; one just keeps on walking, moving, arriving and going. Nor in purely travelling is there plot, or narrative or explanation of or connection found between events. That comes in the stories told – written – about travel. Only in travel writing is there a full stop to mark the end of a journey.

Lismore is perhaps the most spectacular castle in Ireland, theatrically set on a high rock, from which its towers and battlements rear from a froth of trees. It is, if you wish, the Arundel of Ireland, and like Arundel it is a great ducal mansion, the Irish home of the Dukes of Devonshire…Lismore is not altogether what it may first appear, as a discerning eye will perceive. The castle is just a little too good to be true, it has too much of the stage castle and too little of grim reality…The castle rises over the river with tremendous effect and its high towers and wall walks have extensive and beautiful views of the river valley and of distant mountains, views that are alas unfortunately not available to the general public. The next best thing is the view from the bridge below the castle. The bridge was built in 1714; its large arch over the water is echoed by a series of smaller arches that carry the road over a low water-meadow. Upstream or downstream there are excellent and luxuriant views of varied green, with the castle rising overwhelmingly at close quarters on the upstream side. Downstream a widening river passes peacefully through banks of trees and beside level water-meadows towards the Monavullaghs in the east.

Seán Jennett, *Munster*, 1967

Órfhlaith Ní Chonaill

Since my youth I have carried an idyllic memory of bluebells in May beside the Blackwater and the pungent smell of wild garlic as my brother and I sang with friends around a bonfire in the woods beside Lismore Castle. It was my old friend, Catherine Murray, who organised that memorable session over 30 years ago. Nowadays, she and her husband, Jan, are involved in organizing the Immrama Festival. In 2008 I was honoured to be invited back to Lismore to participate in that event.

Independently of each other, Catherine's life and mine had taken us to East Africa, to Tanzania and Kenya respectively. Catherine had read my novel, *The Man With No Skin*, which is set in Kenya. As the theme of Immrama that year was "Africa: Travel and People", I was asked to facilitate a creative writing workshop. So I packed up all my Africana into a box and set off to inspire wonderful writing.

What a joy it was to be in the company of other people who love Africa. I'm not sure that anyone who has ever lived or worked there comes back fully in body and soul. There's always a part of us left behind there, or an Africa that we carry with us that entangles itself in our journeys.

The Africa that I brought home with me contains a young woman at a sewing machine surrounded by colourful cloth; a man wearing shorts and diving to pick leaves out of a hot, green spa pool beside banana trees; Sam, the musician, playing his guitar and singing "Dereva Chunga Maisha waa—aay" (Driver Save Lives) and *Malaika* (Angel); a pub with a tree growing up through the corner of the bar and woven banana leaves for a roof; a St. Patrick's Day when we sang Irish ballads and found that the Kenyans knew all the words; the joy of singing De Dannan's *Mandela is the One* in a Kenyan pub on the night that Nelson Mandela was elected President of South Africa; the story of our friend, Ndohiu, who was in Johannesburg at the time and went out to Soweto to celebrate with his South African brothers, only to be relieved, by them, of his watch and wallet; street children, stinking of glue and excrement, jostling for money on the street; the eerie glow in the sky as a Nairobi shanty suburb (locally known as Soweto) burned to the ground, leaving thousands homeless; cucumber sandwiches after rugby matches in my son's school; the tangy taste of goat-meat roasted over charcoal in the congenial company of Kenyan friends; countless stories recounted with humour and panache; the sense of privilege to have been welcomed into a community and a culture which was so different and yet, in startling ways, so like our own.

A deep connection with Africa was obvious in the other participants in Immrama too. George Alagiah's family had fled from Sri Lanka and found refuge in Ghana. In his address George spoke fondly of his years growing up there and of the great sense of confidence and hope at that time that an Independent Africa could hold its place among equals on the world stage. Despite all his years working as a war correspondent, his message was still one of hope.

On Saturday night Tim Butcher read from his book *Blood River*. He described his journey through war-torn Congo in the footsteps of Stanley. As a pillion passenger on a motorbike, he had travelled along a lost road, abandoned since the war and overgrown by the jungle. He visited villages where only the old remembered seeing motorbikes or cars.

The organizing committee of Immrama treated their guests as VIPs. We were accommodated in the lovely Ballyrafter Country House Hotel. I wasn't allowed to put my hand in my pocket to pay for anything. On the Friday evening myself and Maidhc Dainín Ó Sé were accidentally locked out of the town hall where there was a reading in progress. So we had a pint instead. We recognized each other as fellow Kerry people and writers. It was great to converse in West Kerry Irish and to recall visits to the Gaeltacht in Feoghanach and Dun Chaoin. Maidhc is a mighty storyteller, both in English and Irish. Although as a child he was told he'd never make a scholar, he has written 19 books in Irish, at least one of which is on the Leaving Certificate curriculum.

Of course, no festival would be complete without a music session and we had a great one in the beer garden of a local pub. Maidhc Dainín played his button accordion and I was persuaded to sing a song or two. It amazes me that so much enjoyment was fitted into such a short space of time; although there was so much to do, we were never overburdened. It was easy going and yet the whole weekend ran smoothly and on time.

My Saturday creative writing workshops were in Ballyrafter Country House, in a bright room with a bay window. There was some fabulous writing done there. The participants were from diverse backgrounds and we bonded together as a group, even meeting up for lunch on Sunday. The final workshop was held in the town hall on Sunday morning. I was given a marvellous surprise when Orla from the Immrama committee came in and presented me with a gorgeous piece of Waterford crystal – a replica of the church in Lismore.

The Immram is an enchanted voyage to the otherworld. Africa felt like that for me. And the Immrama festival reconnected me with the enchantment of that world and the long ago world of Lismore and Dun Chaoin. I carry Immrama 2008 with me too as a recent memory, better even than the original idyll. Sometime, I hope to return again as a guest or a participant. And I wish Jan, Catherine, Orla, Mary and all the committee, authors and participants a great new decade of Immrama.

This place is as beautiful and odd as ever. The town is a bit sad, more shops shut, no tourists (longed for by all) because of the fantastic prices & the fact that people think the south of Ireland is the same as the north. Inflation is 23%. You get fewer than four stamps for a £1. It's 26p each, even for a letter to the next village. Goodness knows how people with big families feed their children. It must be as difficult now as it was when the wages were 30/– a week. And so on. No word of R Kee [Robert Kee, author of *Ireland: A History*], but I was sitting in the beautiful new hairdresser's salon (The Golden Scissors) in Main St above Crotty's Bar Best Drinks, wireless full on as per, & a man [Robert Kee] started on about his book & how we must all buy it pronto, well of course...I said to the gardener here It all looks very nice. Ah he said When it's open in the summer *people of all nationalities are charmed with it.*

Letter from Deborah Devonshire to Patrick Leigh Fermor, April 1982
written at Lismore Castle and extracted from *In Tearing Haste,
Letters between Deborah Devonshire and Patrick Leigh Fermor*, 2008
Edited by Charlotte Mosley

Paul Clements

"A place with a different pace," is how the tourist authorities sum up the Blackwater Valley. And the pace of life is what many people who come to Lismore love most about it. Designated in 1991 as a heritage town, it meets the criteria of having 'an inviting cosiness' with a unique character of architectural styles spanning many centuries.

A crossroads town that since 2003 has attracted renowned writers from around the world, Lismore has long been a magnet for statesmen, luminaries and travellers. Gimlet-eyed writers have bestowed many epithets to try to capture its *genius loci*. A few have reflected the sense of timelessness that is felt, something about which visitors often remark, along with its unchanging nature: whispered conversations at crossroads, children playing on the footpaths in the West End, and at the junction of main street and South Mall farmers leaning against the walls as if in conspiracy. By the end of the first decade of the twenty-first century there are no longer any drapery or hardware stores in Lismore – DVD shops, café-bars filled with electro-chatter, chic restaurants and art galleries now look for custom but mercifully some of the time-burnished pubs have survived.

If ever a bar looked inviting, then the Red House Inn on the main street must win the award for Ireland's most eye-catching pub. Built over a century ago, it still retains its original characteristics. With its elegant timber veranda balcony, oriel window, carved timber bargeboards, and red livery, it draws in the newly-arrived visitor. Often, they are to be seen agonizing over which road to take at the Ambrose Power Memorial public drinking fountain (built in 1872 in honour of the former Archdeacon of Lismore) and standing squarely in the town centre.

In architectural parlance the pub makes 'a dramatic visual statement' against the Classical treatment of the courthouse and the hotel. Step into the conviviality and you will meet musicians and storytellers – even thirsty travel writers – holding court and indulging in some West Waterford Weltschmerz. Fiddle-players, accordionists, sean-nós singers, poets and wordspinners have all crossed the door into a place that welcomes the performer. The fun, never mind the drama, of Sunday night's wandering seanchaí James Lenane always delayed my departure until Monday. Just like the wide parameters of travel writing itself, my Immrama weekends have had enormous elasticity, frequently starting around Thursday afternoon and ending on Monday morning.

I have been captured by an unsung part of the country, little-visited as a rule by tourists and a place that is hard to leave. Prime agricultural land rich in dairy farming, its fields are filled with large herds of Charlois cows chomping on lush green grass, and it is redolent of an older slower-paced Ireland. It is an area where – if they come this way at all – tourists race through to somewhere else: Cork city, West Cork, Youghal, the coast at Ardmore, Kerry, or north to the Burren, Galway city or Connemara. They are enamoured by Ireland's tourist traps but those who blink and miss it are losing out on an architectural gem, somewhere that rewards time spent getting to know it and the chance to strike up acquaintance with genuine Lismoreians, amongst the friendliest people you are likely to meet anywhere.

"The Blue Sky Bends Over All" is the Immrama motto. In June the skies over Lismore are generally a dazzling gentian blue, the voluptuous and venerable multi-limbed trees along the Blackwater a forest green; each year the unstoppable rhododendron swathes on the Vee road look a more startling heliotrope than ever while the Red House seems to have a deeper scarlet glow on each visit.

It can be hard to pin down exactly what is so special about Lismore. It is a place of glances, glimpsed views, and secrets tucked down alleyways. Catch the right June day and from a spot on the convent road, often referred to as the back road to Cappoquin, look across rolling countryside and you will enjoy an uninterrupted view of Knockmealdown Mountain, *Cnoc Mhaoldomhnaigh*, the Hill of Moloney or Moloney's Mountain. All around, spring up half a dozen peaks with the moniker 'knock' attached. Wander the hills and valleys, as I have done, and you will discover legends and tales such as that of Petticoat Loose, whom the priests denounced at the altar and who was allegedly banished to the Red Sea; or the story of Major Henry Eeles buried on the summit with his horse, dog and gun because he wanted his last resting place to be nearer heaven.

Scan the Ordnance Survey map and seek out the lyrical townland names: Glenmorrishmeen, Ballyvecane Lower, Ballynelligan, Garrycloyne, Castlerichard Crossroads and Ballymoodranagh. In many passings-through I have often wondered what happens in the small town of Tallow, six miles south of Lismore, a place completely off my Irish topographical radar. Who goes there and why? One of these years, curiosity will get the better of me.

In the decade of Immrama, I have missed only two festivals owing to other commitments. I enjoy the familiarity of old haunts and of finding new ones and being reunited with friends. The hospitable and hard-working committee has rewarded me richly in return. I have launched two travel books on Ireland here and have been involved in talks, workshops, readings, literary breakfasts, round-table discussions, pub crawls and animated conversations on dark and mysterious subjects such as trying to figure out the collective noun for a group of travel writers: a gaggle, a chattering, a glorying, a clamjamfray, a superfluity, an excitement, a farrago? By 2.30 a.m. the jury in the Lismore House Hotel had still not decided, despite invoking much blue-sky thinking. Where is Thackeray when you need him?

The map of Lismore is not big, comprising just a dozen or so streets and lanes running into each other with the North Mall and South Mall linking St. Carthage's Church and St. Carthage's Cathedral. I like wandering the streets, delving into an intriguing entryway, stumbling across a handball alley, discovering a new café, or admiring the built heritage that is remarkable for such a small town. A walk around incorporates a tour of the architectural dictionary covering many centuries. The imprint of the past stands out in the builders' craftsmanship. You will stumble across two-storey Georgian buildings with colourful doors, fan lights and timber framed windows, stone cottages built in the 1820s and 1830s for the estate workers, and a library designed in the Hiberno-Romanesque. Many cottages have kept original decorative features such as canopies or dormers. In some cases the distinctive early sash windows – a common feature in Lismore – still survive.

The place has a wealth of important buildings that would keep an Irish equivalent of Nikolaus Pevsner drooling for a week over lintels, architraves or a rendered fascia. Stretch the geographical boundaries of historic buildings, and you will find Fort William, an astonishing house of sandstone ashlar and the memorable location of a Jan Morris talk that almost came to an abrupt end after rain penetrated the marquee roof. Nearby is the delightful Glencairn Inn, one of many landmark buildings camouflaged in the folds of the countryside, or in the case of Dromana House, perched impressively on a ledge of rock amongst trees, farther along the Blackwater estuary towards Cappoquin.

A deep community pride is taken by locals in the town's appearance. Cottages drip with fuchsia or roses, and each June, as sure as the returning Immrama audience and peripatetic authors, red valerian spreads along Church Lane cascading down the walls.

Window boxes and hanging baskets adorn houses and street lamps, and in the Castle gardens herbaceous borders, magnolias, camellias and foxglove burst forth. The reason for the pristine streets was explained by a shopkeeper who informed me that she was part of a roster of no fewer than 200 people (about one-sixth of the population) tasked to keep the place spick-and-span. Little wonder Lismore has such a distinguished record as a Tidy Towns champion.

Frequently I experience a quickening of the spirit on a riparian ramble along the banks of the Blackwater or by simply pausing on the magnificent seven-arched Cavendish Bridge – with its decorative iron lamp standards – and staring into the currents. High above the river and visible from many vantage-points, the turreted castle – the Irish home of the Dukes of Devonshire since 1753 – towers disproportionately over the town, an imposing and dramatic cynosure. The illustrious guest list has included Sir Edmund Spenser, who is believed to have written part of his epic poem *The Faerie Queene* there. Robert Boyle, the first modern chemist and a key figure in the Scientific Revolution, was born in it in 1627. James II stayed in it after his defeat at the Battle of the Boyne in 1690; and John F. Kennedy, then a young US Congressman, visited in 1947 when he was reunited with his sister Kathleen Harrington.

Every footloose teenager and many travel writers' literary model, Sir Patrick Leigh Fermor was a visitor several times during the second half of the twentieth century. His death coincided with Immrama 2011 when tributes were paid by that year's participants. In the *Guardian* obituary he was memorably described as 'the patron saint of autodidacts'. The eulogies reflected on his time at King's School, Canterbury in the 1920s where he had formed an illicit liaison with the greengrocer's daughter and (in an analogy with the political shenanigans in 2012 Ireland) was sacked for 'conduct unbecoming'. A comment from his housemaster described him as 'a dangerous mixture of sophistication and recklessness'.

My departure from Lismore is generally on public transport to Fermoy, ten miles away, from where I catch a bus to Cork for the flight home. One year outside the Avondhu Bar in Fermoy while waiting for the bus, an elderly woman started a conversation with me. She has lived in Fermoy all her life and asks where I have come from. "Lismore?", she repeats puzzlingly, pronouncing it "Liz-more…I've *heard* of it but I've never been there."

It might as well belong to another continent, or another planet. It could be Samarkand, Kashgar, Paramaribo, Bukhara, Tashkent, Almaty or any of the scores of exotic places that a shelf-load (the correct collective noun) of travel writers has flashed across a blue sky for the people of West Waterford and beyond in the past ten magical years.

Brava Immrama.

"How long will we have you for?" Brother Bonaventura asked. I weathered just two days. The guesthouse was centrally heated and the food was good. In February few casual visitors came – at the time I was the only one. The others were studying for holy orders or were on a retreat. They included a young Seminarist, a couple of Divine Word missionaries, a Professor of Theology and a batch of middle-aged men studying to be priests. It was easier to make a late entry into priesthood than into a contemplative order. "You want to get into those good and early while you're a young man," a late entrant told me. It was difficult enough taking on the life of a priest; he was finding the transition to religious life a lot more difficult than he had anticipated. He had been an army sergeant and getting on when he made the decision, so at least he was used to strictness and routine. I told him that often here in Mount Melleray I was reminded of army life. "What order are you in?" an aspiring priest asked across the breakfast table, and he could almost have been asking what regiment? There was an atmosphere of rank and discipline that suggested an officers' mess.

Peter Somerville-Large, *The Grand Irish Tour*, 1982

Dervla Murphy speaks about her book collection in an interview with Paul Clements recorded at her home in Lismore in June 2003

What place did books have in your life as a child?

"I remember chiefly my grandfather's home in Rathmines in Dublin. It was so filled with books there was scarcely room for people and whatever furniture they had was covered with books. They were arranged in a chaotic manner but to his satisfaction and he could produce any work required at a moment's notice."

What sort of books did he have?

"He had a general range of books including history, philosophy, scriptural commentary, ornithology, and sets of Dickens and Thackeray. I remember he kept the Collected Works of Lord Brougham beside the lavatory. He loved curiosities in books. Some little oddity or one little illustration that struck him as different meant he would buy the book."

Where did he buy books?

"In the 1930s the quays in Dublin were full of secondhand bookshops. When I was a five or six he would often take me with him. To see and touch and smell these books filled me with content and a feeling of joy and security. One set of expensive books that he bought, and that I still own, is a history of the regions of the Italian Republic before Italy was united. It is Sismondi's *Historie des Républiques Italiennes* and was published in an elegantly bound ten-volume set in 1840. He was sent out by his wife to buy a new pair of trousers because he was always reluctant to spend money on new clothes - a trait I have inherited. He saw this edition which cost a considerable amount of money. He didn't buy the trousers but instead bought Sismondi and got a very cool reception from my grandmother when he arrived home still in his threadbare trousers."

Are there any other books of his that are special to you?

"He had a very battered first edition of *A Voyage Round the World* by George Anson from 1748. He bought that for sixpence. It is beautifully illustrated with maps and I still have it in my collection."

How big an influence were your parents in your early reading?

"My father was the County Librarian for Waterford and a bookish man, so I used to spend a lot of time in the library. They had a system of withdrawing books from circulation, some of which went to the fever hospitals. I used to go through the withdrawn ones and pick out whatever I wanted. But it was my mother who encouraged me with the English classics."

What sort of books did she introduce you to?

"She aroused my interest in many of the great writers and in their lives. She had a gift for discussing their characters as if she were gossiping about the neighbours. She immersed herself in the lives of the great. She loved Boswell's *Life of Johnson* which was really her other bible. I became addicted to Shelley, Fielding and Oscar Wilde. I can remember my mother reading *De Profundis* to me. She also had a particular affinity with Jane Austen and George Eliot."

You have written in your autobiography that reading Eliot's *Middlemarch* was amongst the most memorable experiences of your youth, and was 'like watching God creating the world in miniature'. What is it about that book that struck you particularly?

"*Middlemarch* is my favourite novel. It seems to be such a complete world that you are living in. It is the quintessential English novel. It has humour and it makes you think."

What else did you read as a child?

"I was into Just William, Biggles and especially liked Arthur Ransome. As a reader I was a slow developer. I wanted to travel from a young age and my parents gave me an atlas and a bicycle when I was 10. There was another book of my grandfather's with black and white plates of Norway. I used to spend hours just looking at it and imagining I was going on a journey travelling through the mountains and countryside. My parents were very encouraging with birthday and Christmas presents but there was never any pressure on me to read the 'right' books. At the age of 16 I leapt into another world. I was absolutely mad about Ruskin and went on a binge of his work reading *Modern Painters*, *The Stones of Venice* and *Seven Lamps*."

Why did Ruskin capture your imagination?

"I had an irrational reverence for every word he wrote and was grabbed by his style as he is a wonderful writer. Growing up in a small and remote place and reading about Renaissance Italy and the whole philosophy of art was just so exotic and thrilling. It was a totally different world. My grandfather had an American edition called *Ruskin's Works* and by the age of 20 I had read the entire Collected Works."

Could you sum up what you have in the different rooms in the collection in your house?

"My collection is divided into subject matter in different rooms. This room has travel, history and sociology, with books about Ireland occupying one wall. Fiction, biography, sex and Islamic studies are in the bedroom. The lower pagoda, as I call it, houses children's; upstairs is mixum gatherum with books on England, animals and the overflow; the cowhouse has paperback fiction with paperback detective stories in the gallery."

Every country in the world seems represented in your travel books. Whom do you admire in travel writing?

"I love the books of Freya Stark and Patrick Leigh Fermor. The quality of their writing is superb, never mind what they are writing about or the area they are writing about. Their language is beautiful with insightful descriptions of their experiences. I particularly like Freya Stark's *The Valleys of the Assassins* which my mother read to me as a child. It was her second book and came out in 1934 making her name as a writer. As a real adventure story, it stirs the imagination. It chronicles her travels into Luristan, the mountainous terrain between Iraq and present-day Iran, often with only a single guide. She writes engagingly about the nomadic peoples who live in the region's valleys and brings to life their stories. The book also has humour and shows a keen understanding of the people. I have a run of her books, mostly first editions and all signed by her."

Did you know Dame Freya personally?

"I knew her well – she was an amazing person of great charm and was the doyenne of modern travel writers. I met her in the mid-1950s through the legendary Jock Murray, of the famous publishing house. My mother had a few of her early books and I took them over to London to get them autographed. She was a remarkable traveller in the great tradition in her exploration of the far-flung corners of the East."

You quote from Patrick Leigh Fermor's book on Europe several times in your own book on Transylvania. What is it that engages you in his writing?

"I think Leigh Fermor's strengths are the words he uses in such an unusual and wonderful way, and his quirky attitude to things. *Between the Woods and the Water* is one of his best books and I like *A Time To Keep Silence*, which is a graphic account of his stay in a Cistercian Monastery. In his writing he delves into the historical background and describes something that happened perhaps 400 years ago as though he had been there witnessing it. He brings it all to life through his choice of adjectives and the flow of his sentences. The whole scene and panorama opens out before you through his descriptions and especially the colours that he writes about."

Who else do you admire in the travel writing genre?

"Colin Thubron is superb, and for me, *Among the Russians* (1983), is his best book. He learned Russian before he went off on his trip and it's such a help when you can speak the language. I envy that, as it's the key to understanding the people of all kinds that he meets. He covers thousands of miles between the Baltic and Caucasus and the book is a revealing picture of the main races that live in the country. I rate Jan Morris highly too. She has a great ability to recreate somewhere as it was and to evoke the spirit of a place. I much prefer her history books to her travel writing. Her *Pax Britannica* trilogy is magnificent. I also like her book on Venice in 1960, and her book about the sex change, *Conundrum*, was a fascinating read."

I see some books by Paul Theroux and Jonathan Raban. How do you rate their writing?

"I can't stand Theroux - he really switches me off. I just don't like his snide attitude to people. He grumbles and complains too much. But I love Raban's work. Some of his own personality comes out and you feel you like this person. I also like Redmond O'Hanlon – he is an amusing writer meshing in natural history."

Whom do you admire amongst the younger British travel writers?

"I think William Dalrymple is fantastic. He is definitely leading the field amongst the younger generation. He writes gracefully in what is now becoming an old-fashioned style. He is scholarly and entertaining and has an excellent knack of capturing the feel of a place. I also like his humour and how he lightens things."

What is the essence of good quality travel writing?

"It is almost impossible to say. So much depends on the individual traveller and what comes across of the person making the journey."

How has the world of travelling, and travel writing, changed in your lifetime?

"Looking back on 40 years of travelling it is terrifying what has happened to the world with the increase in violence and the deterioration in the political and military scene. Many countries are now too dangerous to visit. For example in Afghanistan you wouldn't get more than 10 yards today before you would be shot or blown up by a mine. I cycled around it alone as a young woman in the Sixties and had no problem. When I went to Ethiopia in the Sixties there were some people living in the Semien Mountains who hadn't seen a white person. Foreigners were not encouraged to travel alone through the remote regions of the country and my highland trek was planned against official advice. When I was trekking in Peru in the Andes there were no motor roads, but most countries now have roads, even in the remotest areas. There are few countries or regions of the world left untapped, but I believe it is still possible for a writer to bring a fresh approach with the right style and an interest in the people."

Which books do you take with you on your travels?

"I don't normally take books that are in anyway related to the country I'm travelling in. But the exception to that was last year when I went to Siberia and took two Dostoevsky novels. I enjoy light easy to read history. Before I go on a journey I read as much as I can as background about the country but not what other travel writers have said about it. I like to know about the history and politics of the country and the social problems. I prefer to have my own impressions not coloured by what other people thought about it."

Do you have a favourite travel book?

"My all time favourite travel book is Mungo Park's *Travels in Africa* first published in 1799. On page two you fall in love with Mungo as he goes off on his intrepid journey into the middle of Africa in search of the Niger where no other white person had been. His descriptions are excellent and his scientific observations have remained of lasting value. He has a completely pre-colonial attitude – there is not a trace of colonialism or imperialism and he takes people as he finds them - as human beings. In the 18th century they really did know how to write. This book has become a classic of travel literature and I have loved it for 50 years."

What is so special about his writing?

"He was so young - he was only about 24 - but he had a great sense of style. He wrote in a straightforward manner providing a unique record of everyday social and domestic life as well as local politics. But the book is also a gripping adventure story. He was courageous, resilient and observant as well as being witty and sensitive. He was a Scotsman and was among the first and greatest of African explorers sent out by the recently founded African Association."

Apart from discursive travel writing, I notice a run of about 40 of the John Murray handbooks in their distinctive red boards. Do you collect these?

"They were given to me by Jock Murray, who was the father of the present owner of the John Murray publishing firm and the sixth of the line. They are exquisitely produced guides from the end of the 19th century. Mine are mostly about the regions of Britain and I have a few European ones. They each have their own folding maps and town plans as well as a quaint section at the back containing Murray's Handbook Advertiser featuring photographs of some of the grand European hotels."

What was Jock Murray like?

"He was an exhilarating mix of the conventional and the eccentric. He was an energetic, generous and inquisitive bookman of the old school. As well as being witty and gracious, he also had great charm and respect for people. In many respects he was my surrogate father. Whenever I was in London I stayed with Jock and his wife Diana, and it was my home from home. As an editorial team they were inspiring."

Could we look at books on specific countries. I see some on Spain – has that always been an interest of yours?

"I was interested in Spain at an early age. I loved Walter Starkie's books, especially *Spanish Raggle-Taggle: Adventures with a Fiddle in North Spain* (1934), about his wanderings in Spain in search of Gypsy music. It was the way I wanted to travel, wandering around with the gypsies, camping out with them, and generally living a vagrant life. I also liked George Borrow's *The Bible in Spain*. I went there three times in the 1950s and felt a great closeness with the Spanish people - it was a fascinating country."

I believe South Africa has interested you for many years?

"My generation was aware of apartheid and I was always interested in the country. I tried to go there in the early eighties but they wouldn't give me a visa. I like the work of André Brink and J. M. Coetzee. I also think Nadine Gordimer is a fabulous writer. Many of her novels wrestle with apartheid and she deals with it in an intelligent and subtle way, not hammering at it."

Asia seems especially well represented with a large number of books on India, Nepal, and Afghanistan; you also have a huge collection on Tibet.

"I'm particularly interested in Tibet although it is so sad about what has happened in the country today. I would have no desire to go there now. During part of 1963 and 1964 I did voluntary work there spending time in Dharamsala and the Kulu Valley. I loved the extraordinary quality of the peasants who were doing the most gruelling manual work. There was a great kindliness about them and it was an amazing culture to have encountered. I visited nursery camps for Tibetan refugee children and met the Dalai Lama. In 1966, my second book, *Tibetan Foothold*, was about my time spent there."

Could you select one book on Tibet that has special resonance?
"There are two in particular. The first is H. E. Richardson's, *Tibet And Its History*, which came out in 1962. It is a lucid history and gives an authoritative overview of Tibetan culture and history. A lot of the early writing romanticized the whole thing and made much of the mystical side of it but Richardson's work is a reliable history. It is detailed but not over-specialized."

Who was he?
"Hugh Richardson was the last British Head of Mission in Lhasa from 1936-1940 and of the Indian Mission from 1947-1950. In 1943 he signed the treaty which gave up British extra-territorial rights in China. In his book he covers the religious kings to the rule of the Dalai Lamas right through to the Communist occupation and the resulting Tibetan rising. Another book that I like is *Secret Tibet* by Fosco Maraini. It is the first modern book on Tibet and is a tremendous travel book with a great translation. It was written in 1952 just before the Communists took over. Maraini lived with local people and travelled with yaks and produced a highly readable book."

Are there any rarities in this section?
"I should mention a two-volume set on Afghanistan that is important to me. It's called *An Account of the Kingdom of Caubul* by the Hon. Mountstuart Elphinstone. My copy is the third revised edition published in 1839. Elphinstone was an Indian statesman and historian who was Governor of Bombay from 1819-1827. He spent some time in Kabul as part of the first British envoy from 1808-1810. Each volume has a colour lithographic frontispiece as well as illustrations and a large folding map. It was one of the first comprehensive surveys of Afghanistan's geography, political history, natural history, social structure and anthropology - although the word probably didn't exist then. It's a marvellous read and includes information on various fringe tribes."

It seems in good condition?
"It was produced in a nice mulberry cloth binding with gilt lettering on the spine. My copy has a bit of wear and tear with some marks but on the whole is good considering its age."

Is there anyone else you admire?
"Another traveller that I like, and who visited Asia, is the 19th century writer Isabella Bird. She covered thousands of miles in the Far East, journeying up the Yangtze Valley, travelling from Baghdad to Teheran, and through Ladakh to Tibet. She also went on horseback through the Rocky Mountains around Colorado and Utah and wrote a memorable book, *A Lady's Life in the Rocky Mountains*."

Travel writing often blends in natural history and anthropology. Are there any books that you want to mention in this category?

"*The Speaking Tree, A Study of Indian Culture and Society*, published in 1971 by Oxford University Press, taught me a huge amount. It is by Richard Lannoy, who lived and worked in India over a period of 20 years. It is a perceptive and analytical study of Indian behaviour, thought and cosmology with the main aim of identifying the origins of the country's contemporary problems. It must be 30 years since I read it and it has given me something that has stayed with me and has become a foundation for developing interests and reading other books on the subject and area."

Your Irish section contains politics, history and biography, as well as travel. What are the highlights here?

"There are many that I have enjoyed immensely. *Jail Journal* by the 19th century Irish revolutionary and historian, John Mitchel, *Guerrilla Days in Ireland* by Tom Barry, and Padraig O'Malley's *The Uncivil Wars* are all excellent books. In history terms I love Roy Foster's *Modern Ireland* which is historical writing at its very best with a compelling literary style. I also like a rather unusual item called *The System of National Education in Ireland* by J. C. Colquhoun, published in 1888. My grandfather had it and something sent me back to it recently. I find it fascinating to read it and think about all the debates that are taking place about education and where Ireland is at post-Celtic tiger."

Is there an Irish book that has special resonance for you?

"I would select *The Village of Longing* by George O'Brien, first published in 1987. It's the story of a childhood in Lismore in the 1950s and is told with great clarity and precision, painting an evocative picture of Irish society. He was brought up in Lismore where his father was the carpenter and he expertly captures the details of everyday life."

I notice a run of Hubert Butler's books. Is he important to you?

"Hubert Butler was neglected for so long but received belated international acclaim. Thankfully, the Lilliput Press in Dublin has republished his works. Butler was born in Kilkenny in 1900 and came from an Anglo-Irish family. He led a rich life of travel, study and strenuous activity on behalf of threatened Jews. He was a teacher in Egypt and the Balkans and travelled later in Asia and America. As a journalist, broadcaster and historian, he was a resolute crusader for honesty in every area of life. In 1990 I wrote the foreword to a collection of his essays *Grandmother and Wolfe Tone*. I described him as one of Ireland's tiny minority of balanced, liberal and fearless thinkers."

He was indeed an outstanding thinker – would you say he had an unadorned prose style?

"He was a beautiful writer and an essayist of remarkable range and talent. Some of his essays have a peculiar moving poignancy; others encourage readers to dose themselves with honesty about modern Ireland and to confront what has gone wrong."

Another book to which you contributed the introduction was George Orwell's *Down and Out in Paris and London*. How did that come about?

"The book was reprinted in the Penguin Classics series in 2001 and I was simply asked by the publishers to write the introduction. It documents Orwell's first contact with poverty when he slept in bug-infested hotels and doss houses, and lived alongside tramps. Orwell was a funny mix in his life, but he remained quite a reactionary in some ways. On his own evidence, he was confused and uncertain. He was obviously a very unhappy man."

***Down and Out in Paris and London* is a work of personalized reportage – how would you assess the strengths of his writing in this book?**

"His writing is a mix of atmosphere and it is a sad book. It has flaws but is oddly endearing. It is the reaction of a sensitive, observant and compassionate young man to poverty and injustice and the callousness of the rich. It offers insights, rather than solutions. He brilliantly documents an area of human experience that his readers could never have glimpsed, or even begun to imagine, without his guidance. In fact, many of his admirers describe it as their favourite Orwell book."

Works of history are well represented on your shelves. Whom would you highlight in this subject area?

"E. P. Thompson's *The Making of the English Working Class* is a brilliant imaginative work of history. Thompson had a great gift for making it seem like a story while you knew it was authentic history - but when it came to riots and political dissension it felt like a novel. It's a long book but you never feel it is a page too long. Another history book that sticks in my mind is *Queen Victoria's Little Wars* by Byron Farwell. It is the story of little-known wars in the North-West Frontier, all over Asia and China, and in Africa and Canada. It is written with a deep understanding and narrative skill, and reflects the bizarre, tragic and often humorous incidents that happened in these small wars."

I notice some titles by writers of dissent, or what might be termed, moral outrage – Noam Chomsky and John Pilger amongst others.

"They both write extremely well. Chomsky is thought-provoking and tells it like it is.

Another area I've latterly become more interested in is the environment and globalisation issues. One book I thorougly recommend is *Our Stolen Future: How man-made chemicals are threatening our fertility, intelligence, and survival.* It is jointly written by Theo Colborn, John Peterson Myers, and Dianne Dumanoski and 30 years of research went into their study. The sub-title sums up the gist of what it is about, but it is petrifying and is a book everyone should read. It is written in a clear popular style and that is a good thing as it means more people will read it than might otherwise if it had been written more scientifically. This text discusses how the relationship between humans and the earth has been disrupted by scientific and technological advances. It lays out emerging scientific data, such as research showing how hormone-disrupting chemicals have derailed sexual development in a host of animals, including humans. It is an indispensable book that is as important as *Silent Spring*, the landmark book by Rachel Carson in the sixties that warned that man-made chemicals had spread across the planet. It is really the follow up to that."

Finally which three books would you take to a desert island?

"I would take Elphinstone's two volumes on Afghanistan. I'd also take *Tom Jones* by Fielding which might cheer me up, and my final choice would be the King James edition of the Bible which would keep me going for a long time."

The village outside the walls of the castle was a pleasant place with a wide street flanked by shops, some of which had windows dressed with merchandise that looked as if it had been acquired in the 1930s. It was early closing and the place was one of the most deserted of all the villages we had so far seen, at least in broad daylight, or what was currently serving as broad daylight in these parts which wasn't much. Even the pub, quite a lively-looking place from the outside, was closed. In every way, in its neatness and well-keptness, Lismore announced itself as something which is still quite common in England wherever Dukes exist but which is almost impossible to credit in Ireland, given the building horrors that have taken place in the last few years: a Ducal appendage.

Eric Newby, *Round Ireland in Low Gear*, 1987

Biographical Notes

Dervla Murphy was born in 1931 in Cappoquin, Co. Waterford. Her first book *Full Tilt: Ireland to India with a Bicycle* was published in 1965. More than 20 others titles have followed, including her acclaimed autobiography *Wheels Within Wheels* (1979). Her travels have taken her through Europe, Africa and Asia. Apart from her travel writing, she has written a number of political or geopolitical books dealing with subjects such as race relations in Britain, the hazards of the nuclear power industry, and the Balkans after the wars in Bosnia and Croatia. She has won worldwide praise for her writing and many awards, including the Christopher Ewart-Biggs Memorial Prize for her book *A Place Apart*.

Tim Butcher is an award-winning journalist, broadcaster and best-selling author. His first book, *Blood River*, used an account of an epic journey he made through the Congo to unravel the region's turbulent history. It was a number one best-seller, translated into six languages and shortlisted for various book prizes. For his second book, *Chasing the Devil*, he trekked 350 miles through Liberia, Guinea and Sierra Leone. On the staff of the *Daily Telegraph* from 1990 to 2009, he specialized in awkward places at awkward times, reporting on conflict in the Balkans, the Middle East and Africa. In 2010 he received an Honorary Doctorate for service as a writer and was made Patron of Save the Congo, a British-based charity. Born in Britain in 1967, he is based in Cape Town with his girlfriend and their two children.

Nuala Hayes is an actor, storyteller and independent radio producer. She trained at the Abbey Theatre and has toured extensively in plays by many of the great Irish playwrights, O'Casey, Synge, Brian Friel and Tom Murphy. Her interest in storytelling began 20 years ago, when she founded Two Chairs Company with musician Ellen Cranitch to explore words and music in performance. Her stories have brought her to many parts of the world. She plays the part of Frankie Byrne, in the hugely successful touring production of 'Dear Frankie' by Niamh Gleeson. She has also launched a CD featuring Irish traditional stories, told by Nuala and Kate Corkery called 'The Brewery of Eggshells.'

Donald Brady was born in Cavan in 1954. He was educated at St. Patrick's College Cavan, NUI Maynooth and UCD. He worked in the public libraries of Dublin, Longford-Westmeath and Clare before his appointment as County Librarian of Waterford, a post he held from 1982 until 2009. His publications include: *The Famine in Waterford*; *The Book of Lismore, an Introduction*; *The illustrious family of the Boyles*, and *Waterford Scientists, Preliminary*

Studies. He is currently working on film and film-making in Waterford and a major study on 19th century Cavan author Mary Anne Sadlier. He has contributed each year to the Immrama programme since his first presentation, Henry Grattan Flood, in 2005.

Áine Uí Fhoghlú, who comes from the Gaeltacht area of An Rinn in Co. Waterford, has written and published poetry, fiction, songs and non-fiction. She has won literary awards including the Michael Hartnett Poetry Prize 2008 and Oireachtas na Gaeilge fiction awards. Her published books are: *Aistear Aonair; An liú sa chuan; Ar an Imeall* (poetry) and *Crúba na Cinniúna; Uisce faoi Thalamh* (fiction).

Pico Iyer is the author of two novels and eight works of non-fiction, including such longtime travellers' favourites as *Video Night in Kathmandu*, *The Lady and the Monk*, *The Global Soul*, *The Open Road* and *The Man Within My Head*. Though he was born and grew up in England, and though he has been to literary festivals from Shanghai to Bogota, he had never set foot in Ireland till Immrama. He has never written about Ireland, but he has hopes.

Thomas McCarthy, who was born in Cappoquin, Co. Waterford in 1954, is the winner of the Patrick Kavanagh Award, The Alice Hunt Bartlett Prize and the Ireland Funds Annual Literary Award. He was educated at the Convent of Mercy, Cappoquin, and at University College, Cork. He has published eight collections of poetry, including *The Lost Province* and *The Last Geraldine Officer*, as well as two novels and a book of essays and memoirs, *Gardens of Remembrance*. A public librarian by profession, he was Fellow of the International Writing Program, University of Iowa, in 1978-79 and Visiting Professor of English at Macalester College, Minnesota in 1994-95. He is a member of Aosdána.

Catherine de Courcy is an Irish writer and historian. She lived in Australia for 16 years and wrote two outback travel books with her late husband, John Johnson. She is an authority on the history of zoos, publishing books and contributing to encyclopaedias and other international publications in Australia, the United States and Ireland. She has also published on other historical topics in Papua New Guinea, Australia and Ireland. She is now a full-time writer and lives in France.

Manchán Magan is a writer and travel documentary-maker based in Ireland. He has written travel books on India, Africa and South America in English and Irish. He has also written plays and novels. He has made over 30 travel documentaries focusing on issues of world culture and globalisation for RTE, TG4, the Travel Channel and History Channel. He writes the *Magan's World* column for *The Irish Times*.

The Blue Sky Bends Over All

Hadani Ditmars is a Lebanese-Canadian author, journalist, and photographer who has reported for two decades from the Middle East. She frequently examines the human costs of sectarian strife as well as cultural resistance to war, occupation and embargo. Her work has been featured in the *New York Times*, the *Guardian* and on the BBC, and she is the author of the *Wallpaper Vancouver City Guide*. A former editor at *New Internationalist*, she travelled to Baghdad to write and photograph a special issue on Iraq in 2010 that included visits to important architectural sites as well as dispatches from the Iraqi National Theatre and the last two remaining art galleries in Baghdad. *Dancing in the No Fly Zone* recounts her time in Iraq from 1997 until late 2003. Her new book, *Ancient Heart*, is a political journey through seven historical sites in Iraq.

Michael Shapiro is a writer and editor based in Sonoma County, just north of San Francisco. He's the author of *A Sense of Place*, a collection of interviews with the world's top travel writers, including Jan Morris, Bill Bryson and Paul Theroux. He wrote a cover story in 2006 on Jan Morris' corner of Wales for *National Geographic Traveler*, covered Mongolia's Naadam Games for the *Washington Post*, and watched devils burn in Guatemala for *American Way*. His story about Lismore, Dervla Murphy, and Immrama appeared in the online travel magazine *Perceptive Travel*.

Alan Murphy is a Dublin-born author and illustrator of two books, *The Mona Lisa's on our Fridge*, reviewed by Robert Dunbar as one of the best children's poetry books of 2009, and *Psychosilly*, which was on an *Irish Times* book list ("Must-reads for under 12s"). He has exhibited his paintings and collages in various locations throughout Ireland and given readings of his poetry at Poetry Now, the West Cork Literary Festival, Immrama and other festivals. He lives in Lismore.

Jan Morris, who was born in 1926, has written some 40 books of history, travel, memoir and imagination. After Oxford she spent ten years as a foreign correspondent, first for *The Times*, then the *Guardian*, and was the only reporter with the expedition that first climbed Everest in 1953. She is an ardent Welsh patriot, and lives with her life's partner Elizabeth and her Norwegian cat Ibsen in the top left corner of Cymru.

Damien Lewis was a war reporter and cameraman for 20 years, working largely for the Frontline Agency and major world broadcasters. He's an internationally bestselling author published in some 30 languages, and writes non-fiction memoirs, military history, travel books and thrillers. He lives in West Cork with his wife and three young children, and occasionally still goes to the odd war zone when his wife will allow him.

Annie G. Rogers is the author of *A Shining Affliction*, and *The Unsayable: The Hidden Language of Trauma*. She is the editor of *Charlie's Chasing the Sheep* and has written memoir, short fiction and poetry. She is Professor of Psychoanalysis and Clinical Psychology at Hampshire College in Amherst, Massachusetts. Annie lives in Lismore with her partner Íde B. O'Carroll, during Christmas and summer breaks.

Jasper Winn is a writer and broadcaster. Brought up in West Cork, his early 'slow adventures' include cycling across the Sahara, West Africa and India, following pilgrimage routes worldwide on foot, kayaking the Danube in East Bloc days and long horse trips on five continents. Jasper lived for a year with nomadic Berbers in North Africa and his experience of working with traditional horse cultures around the globe led to him becoming story consultant on the IMAX cowboy film 'Ride Around the World'. He has made radio and television documentaries for RTE and the BBC. His book, *Paddle; A long way around Ireland* is an account of sea-kayaking the thousand miles around Ireland's coastline.

Órfhlaith Ní Chonaill M. Phil. (Creative Writing) is a writer and facilitator of creative writing workshops using the Amherst Writers & Artists method. Originally from Tralee, Co. Kerry, she now lives in Sligo. Her African novel, *The Man With No Skin* was the recipient of IPPY (Independent Book Publishers') and CIPA (Colorado Independent Publishers) Awards in the US. A short story, *Kikuyu Grass*, was shortlisted for a Hennessy Award and her poems and short stories have been published in *Force 10* and other publications. She has also written a historical novel called *Never in a War*.

Paul Clements is the author of three discursive travel books about Ireland: *Irish Shores, A Journey round the Rim of Ireland* (1993), *The Height of Nonsense, The Ultimate Irish Road Trip* (2005), and *Burren Country, Travels through an Irish limestone landscape* (2011). A former BBC journalist and assistant news editor, he is a contributor to a range of newspapers and magazines including *The Irish Times* and is a regular visitor to Immrama. He has written a critical study of Jan Morris published by the University of Wales Press, and in 2006 edited a Festschrift in honour of her 80th birthday, *Jan Morris: Around the World in Eighty Years*. Since 2008 he has been a contributing writer to *Fodor's Ireland* and *Insight Guide Ireland*. He is a Fellow of Green College, Oxford and lives in Belfast.

Individual and group participants in the
Immrama Travel Writing Festival 2003-2011

AIB Choral Society
Aine Goggins
Áine Uí Fhoghlú
Alan Murphy
Alex von Tunzelmann
Alexandra Tolstoy
An Solas Dubh
Annie G. Rogers
Annie Roper
Booley House
Brian Keenan
Brid Rodgers
Bui Bolg
Carouse
Cathal Ó Searcaigh
Catherine de Courcy
Charlie Bird
Christina Lamb
Conor O'Clery
Corina Duyn
Damien Lewis
Darina Gibson
Darragh Doyle
David Monagan
Declan Hassett
Dermot Somers
Dervla Murphy
Dick Warner
Donal Brady
Fergal Keane
Frank Reidy
Galway Circus Project
George Alagiah
Grace Wells
Guillaume Bonn
Hadani Ditmars
Hullabaloo
Jan Morris
Jane Hughes
Jasper Winn

Jon Halliday
Julian Walton
Jung Chang
Kate Adie
Liam Ó Muirthile
Loudest Whisper
Louis de Paor
Maidhc Dainín O Sé
Manchán Magan
Margaret Ward
Martin Manseragh
Mary Branley
Michael Palin
Motema
Nick Danziger
Nick Middleton
Nuala Hayes
Órfhlaith Ní Chonaill
Paul Clements
Pico Iyer
Pippa Sweeney
Pól Ó Conghaile
Redmond O'Hanlon
Robert Fisk
Rolf Potts
Ronan Browne
Rory Maclean
Sara Wheeler
Sir Ranulph Fiennes
Sir Richard Staples
The Gentlemen of Hereford
The Madhatters
Theo Dorgan
Thomas McCarthy
Tim Butcher
Tim Pat Coogan
Tim Severin
William Beare
William Blacker
Wobbly Circus